BOOKS PUBLISHED

IN BLUE AND GOLD, BY

TICKNOR AND FIELDS.

Longfellow's Poems. 2 vols.
Longfellow's Prose. 2 vols.
Whittier's Poems. 2 vols.
Leigh Hunt's Poems. 2 vols.
Tennyson's Poems. 2 vols.
Gerald Massey's Poems.
Lowell's Poems. 2 vols.
Percival's Poems. 2 vols.
Motherwell's Poems.
Owen Meredith's Poems.
Owen Meredith's Lucile.
Sydney Dobell's Poems.
Bowring's Matins and Vespers.
Allingham's Poems.
Horace. Translated by Theodore Martin.
Mrs. Jameson's Characteristics of Women.
Mrs. Jameson's Loves of the Poets.
Mrs. Jameson's Diary.
Mrs. Jameson's Sketches of Art.
Mrs. Jameson's Legends of the Madonna.
Mrs. Jameson's Italian Painters.
Mrs. Jameson's Studies and Stories.
Saxe's Poems.
Clough's Poems.
Holmes's Poems.
Adelaide Procter's Poems.

POEMS

BY

JOHN G. SAXE.

COMPLETE IN ONE VOLUME.

THIRTY-SECOND EDITION.

BOSTON:
TICKNOR AND FIELDS.
1866.

University Press, Cambridge:
Stereotyped and Printed by Welch, Bigelow, & Co.

CONTENTS.

PROGRESS, AND OTHER POEMS.

THE MONEY-KING, AND OTHER POEMS.

PROGRESS,

AND

OTHER POEMS.

TO HON. GEORGE P. MARSH,

UNITED STATES MINISTER RESIDENT AT CONSTANTINOPLE.

DEAR SIR: —

I dedicate this little Volume to you, not in your capacity as the honored Representative of your country at a Foreign Court, nor yet in your higher character, as one of the foremost scholars of the age; but rather, as is more befitting, in token of my esteem for your private virtues, and in grateful acknowledgment of your personal friendship. I hesitate less to avail myself of your kind permission to use your name in this place, since it was greatly owing to your flattering judgment of my first elaborate essay at verse writing, that other pieces were subsequently undertaken, and that these are now here collected. In christening the book, I have chosen, for several reasons, to conform to the customary nomenclature which allows every kind of literature to be 'Poetry,' that is not written in the fashion of prose; yet I have no quarrel with that nicer rule of modern criticism which assigns to all metrical compositions of a mainly facetious or satirical character, a place rather on the border than fairly within the domain of legitimate poesy. If I have excluded several trifles which some of my friends would like to have seen with the rest, it was because I could not afford to make the volume larger at any risk of making it worse. Should the verses which I have ventured to retain, receive, in their present form, the favor which has been accorded to most of the poems separately, I am very sure no one will be more gratified than yourself, — except it be

Your sincere friend, and humble servant,

JOHN GODFREY SAXE.

BURLINGTON, VERMONT, 1849.

PROGRESS:

A SATIRE.

In this, our happy and 'progressive' age,
When all alike ambitious cares engage;
When beardless boys to sudden sages grow,
And 'Miss' her nurse abandons for a beau;
When for their dogmas Non-Resistants fight,
When dunces lecture, and when dandies write
When, martial honors to the children thrown,
Each five-foot minor is a 'Major' grown;
When matrons, seized with oratoric pangs,
Give happy birth to masculine harangues,
And spinsters, trembling for the nation's fate,
Neglect their stockings to preserve the State;
When critic-wits their brazen lustre shed
On golden authors whom they never read,
With parrot praise of 'Roman grandeur' speak,
And in bad English eulogize the Greek;—
When facts like these no reprehension bring,
May not, uncensured, an Attorney sing?
In sooth he may; and though 'unborn' to climb
Parnassus' heights, and 'build the lofty rhyme,'

Though FLACCUS fret, and warningly advise
That 'middling verses gods and men despise,'
Yet will he sing, to Yankee license true,
In spite of Horace and 'Minerva' too!

My theme is PROGRESS, — never-tiring theme
Of prosing dulness, and poetic dream;
Beloved of Optimists, who still protest
Whatever happens happens for the best;
Who prate of 'evil' as a thing unknown,
A fancied color, or a seeming tone,
A vague chimera cherished by the dull,
The empty product of an emptier skull.
Expert logicians they! — to show at will,
By ill philosophy, that naught is ill!
Should some sly rogue, the city's constant curse,
Deplete your pocket and relieve your purse,
Or if, approaching with ill-omened tread,
Some bolder burglar break your house and head,
Hold, friend, thy rage! nay, let the rascal flee;
No evil has been done the world, or thee:
Here comes Philosophy will make it plain
Thy seeming loss is universal gain!
'Thy heap of gold was clearly grown too great, —
'T were best the poor should share thy large estate
While misers gather, that the knaves should steal,
Is most conducive to the general weal;
Thus thieves the wrongs of avarice efface,
And stand the friends and stewards of the race;
Thus every moral ill but serves, in fact,
Some other equal ill to counteract.'

Sublime Philosophy! — benignant light!
Which sees in every pair of wrongs, a right;
Which finds no evil or in sin or pain,
And proves that decalogues are writ in vain!

Hail, mighty PROGRESS! — loftiest we find
Thy stalking strides in science of the mind.
What boots it now that LOCKE was learned and wise?
What boots it now that men have ears and eyes?
'Pure Reason' in their stead now hears and sees,
And walks apart in stately scorn of these;
Laughs at 'experience,' spurns 'induction' hence,
Scouting 'the senses,' and transcending sense.
No more shall flippant ignorance inquire,
'If German breasts may feel poetic fire,'
Nor German dulness write ten folios full,
To show, for once, that Dutchmen are not dull.[1]
For here Philosophy, acute, refined,
Sings all the marvels of the human mind
In strains so passing 'dainty sweet' to hear,
That e'en the nursery turns a ravished ear!
Here Wit and Fancy in scholastic bowers
Twine beauteous wreaths of metaphysic flowers;
Here Speculation pours her dazzling light,
Here grand Invention wings a daring flight,
And soars ambitious to the lofty moon,
Whence, haply, freighted with some precious boon,
Some old 'Philosophy' in fog incased,
Or new 'Religion' for the changing taste,
She straight descends to Learning's blest abodes,
Just simultaneous with the Paris modes!

Here PLATO's dogmas eloquently speak,
Not as of yore, in grand and graceful Greek,
But, (quite beyond the dreaming sage's hope
Of future glory in his fancy's scope,)
Translated *down*, as by some wizard touch,
Find 'immortality' in good high Dutch!

Happy the youth, in this our golden age,
Condemned no more to con the prosy page
Of LOCKE and BACON, antiquated fools,
Now justly banished from our moral schools.
By easier modes philosophy is taught,
Than through the medium of laborious thought.
Imagination kindly serves instead,
And saves the pupil many an aching head.
Room for the sages! — hither comes a throng
Of blooming Platos trippingly along.
In dress how fitted to beguile the fair!
What intellectual, stately heads — of hair!
Hark to the Oracle! — to Wisdom's tone
Breathed in a fragrant zephyr of Cologne.
That boy in gloves, the leader of the van,
Talks of the 'outer' and the 'inner man,'
And knits his girlish brow in stout resolve
Some mountain-sized 'idea' to 'evolve.'
Delusive toil! — thus in their infant days,
When children mimic manly deeds in plays,
Long will they sit, and eager 'bob for whale'
Within the ocean of a water-pail!
The next, whose looks unluckily reveal
The ears portentous that his locks conceal,

Prates of the 'orbs' with such a knowing frown,
You deem he puffs some lithographic town
In Western wilds, where yet unbroken ranks
Of thrifty beavers build unchartered 'banks,'
And prowling panthers occupy the lots
Adorned with churches on the paper plots!
But ah! what suff'ring harp is this we hear?
What jarring sounds invade the wounded ear?
Who o'er the lyre a hand spasmodic flings,
And grinds harsh discord from the tortured strings?
The Sacred Muses, at the sound dismayed,
Retreat disordered to their native shade,
And PHŒBUS hastens to his high abode,
And ORPHEUS frowns to hear an 'Orphic ode'!

Talk not, ye jockeys, of the wondrous speed
That marks your Northern or your Southern steed
See Progress fly o'er Education's course!
Not far-famed Derby owns a fleeter horse!
On rare Improvement's 'short and easy' road,
How swift her flight to Learning's blest abode!
In other times — 't was many years ago —
The scholar's course was toilsome, rough, and slow,
The fair Humanities were sought in tears,
And came, the trophy of laborious years.
Now Learning's shrine each idle youth may seek,
And, spending there a shilling and a week,
(At lightest cost of study, cash, and lungs,)
Come back, like *Rumor*, with a hundred tongues!

What boots such progress, when the golden load
From heedless haste is lost upon the road?

When each great science, to the student's pace,
Stands like the wicket in a hurdle race,
Which to o'erleap is all the courser's mind,
And all his glory that 't is left behind!

Nor less, O Progress, are thy newest rules
Enforced and honored in the 'Ladies' Schools;'
Where Education, in its nobler sense,
Gives place to Learning's shallowest pretence;
Where hapless maids, in spite of wish or taste,
On vain 'accomplishments' their moments waste;
By cruel parents here condemned to wrench
Their tender throats in mispronouncing French;
Here doomed to force, by unrelenting knocks,
Reluctant music from a tortured box;
Here taught, in inky shades and rigid lines,
To perpetrate equivocal 'designs;'
'Drawings' that prove their title plainly true,
By showing nature 'drawn,' and 'quartered' too!
In ancient times, I've heard my grandam tell,
Young maids were taught to read, and write, and spell;
(Neglected arts! once learned by rigid rules,
As prime essentials in the 'common schools;')
Well taught beside in many a useful art
To mend the manners and improve the heart;
Nor yet unskilled to turn the busy wheel,
To ply the shuttle, and to twirl the reel,
Could thrifty tasks with cheerful grace pursue,
Themselves 'accomplished,' and their duties too.
Of tongues, each maiden had but one, 't is said,
(Enough, 't was thought, to serve a lady's head,)

But that was ENGLISH, — great and glorious tongue
That CHATHAM spoke, and MILTON, SHAKSPEARE, sung!
Let thoughts too idle to be fitly dressed
In sturdy Saxon, be in French expressed;
Let lovers breathe Italian, — like, in sooth,
Its singers, soft, emasculate, and smooth;
But for a tongue whose ample powers embrace
Beauty and force, sublimity and grace,
Ornate or plain, harmonious, yet strong,
And formed alike for eloquence and song,
Give me the ENGLISH, — aptest tongue to paint
A sage or dunce, a villain or a saint,
To spur the slothful, counsel the distressed,
To lash the oppressor, and to soothe the oppressed,
To lend fantastic Humor freest scope
To marshal all his laughter-moving troop,
Give Pathos power, and Fancy lightest wings,
And Wit his merriest whims and keenest stings!

The march of Progress let the Muse explore
In pseudo-science and empiric lore.
O sacred Science! how art thou profaned,
When shallow quacks and vagrants, unrestrained,
Flaunt in thy robes, and vagabonds are known
To brawl thy name, who never wrote their own;
When crazy theorists their addled schemes
(Unseemly product of dyspeptic dreams)
Impute to thee! — as courtesans of yore
Their spurious bantlings left at Mars's door;
When each projector of a patent pill,
Or happy founder of a coffee-mill,

Invokes thine aid to celebrate his wares,
And crown with gold his philanthropic cares;
Thus Islam's hawkers piously proclaim
Their figs and pippins in the Prophet's name!

Some sage Physician, studious to advance
The art of healing, and its praise enhance,
By observation 'scientific' finds
(What else were hidden from inferior minds)
That WATER's useful in a thousand ways,
To cherish health, and lengthen out our days:
A mighty solvent in its simple scope,
And quite 'specific' with Castilian soap!
The doctor's labors let the thoughtless scorn,
See! a new 'science' to the world is born;
'Disease is dirt! all pain the patient feels
Is but the soiling of the vital wheels;
To wash away all particles impure,
And cleanse the system, plainly is to cure!'
Thus shouts the doctor, eloquent, and proud
To teach his 'science' to the gaping crowd;
Like 'Father Mathew,' eager to allure
Afflicted mortals to his 'water-cure'!

'T is thus that modern 'sciences' are made,
By bold assumption, puffing, and parade.
Take three stale 'truths;' a dozen 'facts,' assumed;
Two known 'effects,' and fifty more presumed;
'Affinities' a score, to sense unknown,
And, just as '*lucus, non lucendo*' shown,

Add but a name of pompous Anglo-Greek,
And only not impossible to speak,
The work is done; a 'science' stands confest,
And countless welcomes greet the queenly guest

In closest girdle, O reluctant Muse,
In scantiest skirts, and lightest-stepping shoes,[2]
Prepare to follow FASHION'S gay advance,
And thread the mazes of her motley dance;
And, marking well each momentary hue,
And transient form, that meets the wondering view
In kindred colors, gentle Muse, essay
Her Protean phases fitly to portray.
To-day, she slowly drags a cumbrous trail,
And 'Ton' rejoices in its length of tail;
To-morrow, changing her capricious sport,
She trims her flounces just as much too short;
To-day, right jauntily, a hat she wears
That scarce affords a shelter to her ears;
To-morrow, haply, searching long in vain,
You spy her features down a Leghorn lane;
To-day, she glides along with queenly grace,
To-morrow ambles in a mincing pace.
To-day, erect, she loves a martial air,
And envious train-bands emulate the fair;
To-morrow, changing as her whim may serve,
'She stoops to conquer' in a 'Grecian curve.'[3]
To-day, with careful negligence arrayed
In scanty folds, of woven zephyrs made,
She moves like Dian in her woody bowers,
Or Flora floating o'er a bed of flowers;

To-morrow, laden with a motley freight,
Of startling bulk and formidable weight,
She waddles forth, ambitious to amaze
The vulgar crowd, who giggle as they gaze!

Despotic Fashion! potent is her sway,
Whom half the world full loyally obey,
Kings bow submissive to her stern decrees,
And proud Republics bend their necks and knees;
Where'er we turn the attentive eye, is seen
The worshipped presence of the modish queen;
In Dress, Philosophy, Religion, Art,
Whate'er employs the head, or hand, or heart.

Is some fine lady quite o'ercome with woes,
From an unyielding pimple on her nose,—
Some unaccustomed 'buzzing in her ears,'
Or other marvel to alarm her fears?
Fashion, with skill and judgment ever nice,
At once advises 'medical advice;'
Then names her doctor, who, arrived in haste,
Proceeds accordant with the laws of taste.
If real ills afflict the modish dame,
Her blind idolatry is still the same;
Less grievous far, she deems it, to endure
Genteel malpractice, than a vulgar cure.
If, spite of gilded pills and golden fees,
Her dear dyspepsia grows a dire disease,
And Docter DAPPER proves a shallow rogue,
The world must own that both were much in vogue

What impious mockery, when, with soulless art,
Fashion, intrusive, seeks to rule the heart;

Directs how grief may tastefully be borne;
Instructs Bereavement just how long to mourn;
Shows Sorrow how by nice degrees to fade,
And marks its measure in a ribbon's shade!
More impious still, when, through her wanton laws,
She desecrates Religion's sacred cause;
Shows how 'the narrow road' is easiest trod,
And how, genteelest, worms may worship God;
How sacred rites may bear a worldly grace,
And self-abasement wear a haughty face;
How sinners, long in Folly's mazes whirled,
With pomp and splendor may 'renounce the world;
How 'with all saints hereafter to appear,'
Yet quite escape the vulgar portion here!

Imperial Fashion! her impartial care
Things most momentous, and most trivial, share.
Now crushing conscience (her invet'rate foe),
And now a waist, and now, perchance, a toe;
At once for pistols and 'the Polka' votes,
And shapes alike our characters and coats;
The gravest question which the world divides,
And lightest riddle, in a breath decides:
'If wrong may not, by circumstance, be right,'—
'If black cravats be more genteel than white,'—
'If by her "bishop," or her "grace," alone,
A genuine lady, or a church, is known;'—
Problems like these she solves with graceful air,
At once a casuist and a connoisseur!

Does some sleek knave, whom magic money-bags
Have raised above his fellow-knaves in rags,

Some willing minion of unblushing Vice,
Who boasts that 'Virtue ever has her price,'—
Does he, unpitying, blast thy sister's fame,
Or doom thy daughter to undying shame,
To bow her head beneath the eye of scorn,
And droop and wither in her maiden morn?
Fashion 'regrets,' declares ''t was very wrong,'
And, quite dejected, hums an opera song!
Impartial friend! your cause to her appealed,
Yourself and foe she summons to the field,
Where Honor carefully the case observes,
And nicely weighs it in a scale of nerves!
Despotic rite! whose fierce vindictive reign
Boasts, unrebuked, its countless victims slain,
While Christian rulers, recreant, support
The pagan honors of thy bloody court,
And 'Freedom's champions' spurn their hallowed trust,
Kneel at thy nod, and basely lick the dust!

Degraded Congress! once the honored scene
Of patriot deeds; where men of solemn mien,
In virtue strong, in understanding clear,
Earnest, though courteous, and, though smooth, sincere,
To gravest counsels lent the teeming hours,
And gave their country all their mighty powers.
But times are changed; a rude, degenerate race
Usurp the seats, and shame the sacred place.
Here plotting demagogues, with zeal defend
The 'people's rights,'—to gain some private end;

Here Southern youths, on Folly's surges tost,
Their fathers' wisdom eloquently boast;
(So dowerless spinsters proudly number o'er
The costly jewels that their grandams wore.)
Here would-be TULLYS pompously parade
Their tumid tropes for simple 'Buncombe' made,[4]
Full on the chair the chilling torrent shower,
And work their word-pumps through the allotted
hour.
Deluded 'Buncombe!' while, with honest praise,
She notes each grand and patriotic phrase,
And, much rejoicing in her hopeful son,
Deems all her own the laurels he has won,
She little dreams how brother members fled,
And left the house as vacant as his head!
Here rural CHATHAMS, eager to attest
The 'growing greatness of the mighty West,'
To make the plainest proposition clear,
Crack PRISCIAN'S head, and Mr. SPEAKER'S ear;
Then, closing up in one terrific shout,
Pour all their 'wild-cats' furiously out!
Here lawless boors with ruffian bullies vie,
Who last shall give the rude, insulting 'lie,'
While 'Order! order!' loud the chairman calls,
And echoing 'Order!' every member bawls;
Till rising high in rancorous debate,
And higher still in fierce envenomed hate,[5]
Retorted blows the scene of riot crown,
And big LYCURGUS knocks the lesser down!

Ye honest dames in frequent proverbs named,
For finest fish and foulest English famed,
Whose matchless tongues, 'tis said, were never heard
To speak a flattering or a feeble word, —
Here all your choice invective ye might urge
Our lawless *Solons* fittingly to scourge;
Here, in congenial company, might rail
Till, quite worn out, your creaking voices fail, —
Unless, indeed, for once compelled to yield
In wordy strife, ye vanquished quit the field!

Hail, Social Progress! each new moon is rife
With some new theory of social life,
Some matchless scheme ingeniously designed
From half their miseries to free mankind;
On human wrongs triumphant war to wage,
And bring anew the glorious golden age.
'Association' is the magic word
From many a social 'priest and prophet' heard,
'Attractive Labor' is the angel given,
To render earth a sublunary Heaven!
'Attractive Labor!' ring the changes round,
And labor grows attractive in the sound;
And many a youthful mind, where haply lurk
Unwelcomed fancies at the name of 'work,'
Sees pleasant pastime in its longing view
Of 'toil made easy' and 'attractive' too,
And, fancy-rapt, with joyful ardor, turns
Delightful grindstones and seductive churns!
'Men are not bad,' these social sages preach,
'Men are not what their actions seem to teach,

No moral ill is natural or fixed, —
Men only err by being badly mixed!'
To them the world a huge plum-pudding seems,
Made up of richest viands, fruits, and creams,
Which of all choice ingredients partook,
And then was ruined by a blundering cook!

Inventive France! what wonder-working schemes
Astound the world whene'er a Frenchman dreams
What fine-spun theories, — ingenious, new,
Sublime, stupendous, everything but true!
One little favor, O 'Imperial France'!
Still teach the world to cook, to dress, to dance;
Let, if thou wilt, thy boots and barbers roam,
But keep thy morals and thy creeds at home!

O might the Muse prolong her flowing rhyme,
(Too closely cramped by unrelenting Time,
Whose dreadful scythe swings heedlessly along,
And, missing speeches, clips the thread of song,)
How would she strive, in fitting verse, to sing
The wondrous Progress of the Printing King!
Bibles and Novels, Treatises and Songs,
Lectures on 'Rights,' and Strictures upon Wrongs;
Verse in all metres, Travels in all climes,
Rhymes without reason, Sonnets without rhymes;
'Translations from the French,' so vilely done,
The wheat escaping leaves the chaff alone;
Memoirs, where dunces sturdily essay
To cheat Oblivion of her certain prey;
Critiques, where pedants vauntingly expose
Unlicensed verses, in unlawful prose;

Lampoons, whose authors strive in vain to throw
Their headless arrows from a nerveless bow;
Poems by youths, who, crossing Nature's will,
Harangue the landscape they were born to till;
Huge tomes of Law, that lead by rugged routes
Through ancient dogmas down to modern doubts;
Where Judges oft, with well-affected ease,
Give learned reasons for absurd decrees,
Or, more ingenious still, contrive to found
Some just decision on fallacious ground,
Or blink the point, and, haply, in its place,
Moot and decide some hypothetic case;
Smart Epigrams, all sadly out of joint,
And pointless, — save the 'exclamation point,
Which stands in state, with vacant wonder fraught,
The pompous tombstone of some pauper thought;
Ingenious systems based on doubtful facts,
'Tracts for the Times,' and most untimely tracts;
Polemic Pamphlets, Literary Toys,
And Easy Lessons for uneasy boys;
Hebdomadal Gazettes, and Daily News,
Gay Magazines, and Quarterly Reviews; —
Small portion these, of all the vast array
Of darkened leaves that cloud each passing day
And pour their tide unceasingly along,
A gathering, swelling, overwhelming throng!

Cease, O my Muse, nor, indiscreet, prolong
To epic length thy unambitious song.
Good friends, be gentle to a maiden Muse,
Her errors pardon, and her faults excuse.

Not uninvited to her task she came,[6]
To sue for favor, not to seek for fame.
Be this, at least, her just though humble praise:
No stale excuses heralded her lays,
No singer's trick, — conveniently to bring
A sudden cough, when importuned to sing;[7]
No deprecating phrases, learned by rote,' —
'She 'd quite forgot,' or 'never knew a note,' —
But to her task, with ready zeal, addressed
Her earnest care, and aimed to do her best;
Strove to be just in each satiric word,
To doubtful wit undoubted truth preferred,
To please and profit equally has aimed,
Nor been ill-natured even when she blamed.

THE PROUD MISS MAC BRIDE:

A LEGEND OF GOTHAM.

I.

O, TERRIBLY proud was Miss Mac Bride,
The very personification of Pride,
As she minced along in Fashion's tide,
Adown Broadway, — on the proper side, —
        When the golden sun was setting;
There was pride in the head she carried so high,
Pride in her lip, and pride in her eye,
And a world of pride in the very sigh
        That her stately bosom was fretting;

II.

A sigh that a pair of elegant feet,
Sandalled in satin, should kiss the street, —
The very same that the vulgar greet
In common leather not over 'neat,' —
        For such is the common booting;
(And Christian tears may well be shed,
That even among our gentlemen bred,
The glorious day of Morocco is dead,
And Day and Martin are raining instead,
        On a much inferior footing!)

III.

O, terribly proud was Miss Mac Bride,
Proud of her beauty, and proud of her pride,
And proud of fifty matters beside
    That would n't have borne dissection;
Proud of her wit, and proud of her walk,
Proud of her teeth, and proud of her talk,
Proud of 'knowing cheese from chalk,'
    On a very slight inspection!

IV.

Proud abroad, and proud at home,
Proud wherever she chanced to come,
When she was glad, and when she was glum;
    Proud as the head of a Saracen
Over the door of a tippling shop!—
Proud as a duchess, proud as a fop,
'Proud as a boy with a bran-new top,'
    Proud beyond comparison!

V.

It seems a singular thing to say,
But her very senses led her astray
    Respecting all humility;
In sooth, her dull auricular drum
Could find in *Humble* only a 'hum,'
And heard no sound of 'gentle' come,
    In talking about gentility.

VI.

What *Lowly* meant she did n't know,
For she always avoided 'everything low,'

With care the most punctilious,
And queerer still, the audible sound
Of 'super-silly' she never had found
In the adjective supercilious!

VII.

The meaning of *Meek* she never knew,
But imagined the phrase had something to do
With 'Moses,' — a peddling German Jew,
Who, like all hawkers the country through,
Was a person of no position;
And it seemed to her exceedingly plain,
If the word was really known to pertain
To a vulgar German, it was n't germane
To a lady of high condition!

VIII.

Even her graces, — not her grace,
For that was in the 'vocative case,' —
Chilled with the touch of her icy face,
Sat very stiffly upon her;
She never confessed a favor aloud,
Like one of the simple, common crowd,
But coldly smiled, and faintly bowed,
As who should say: 'You do me proud,
And do yourself an honor!'

IX.

And yet the pride of Miss Mac Bride,
Although it had fifty hobbies to ride,
Had really no foundation;

But, like the fabrics that gossips devise,—
Those single stories that often arise
And grow till they reach a four-story size,—
Was merely a fancy creation!

X.

'T is a curious fact as ever was known
In human nature, but often shown
Alike in castle and cottage,
That pride, like pigs of a certain breed,
Will manage to live and thrive on 'feed'
As poor as a pauper's pottage!

XI.

That her wit should never have made her vain,
Was, like her face, sufficiently plain;
And as to her musical powers,
Although she sang until she was hoarse,
And issued notes with a Banker's force,
They were just such notes as we never indorse
For any acquaintance of ours!

XII.

Her birth, indeed, was uncommonly high,
For Miss Mac Bride first opened her eye
Through a sky-light dim, on the light of the sky;
But pride is a curious passion,
And in talking about her wealth and worth,
She always forgot to mention her birth,
To people of rank and fashion!

2

XIII.

Of all the notable things on earth,
The queerest one is pride of birth,
Among our 'fierce Democracie'!
A bridge across a hundred years,
Without a prop to save it from sneers, —
Not even a couple of rotten Peers, —
A thing for laughter, fleers, and jeers,
Is American aristocracy!

XIV.

English and Irish, French and Spanish,
German, Italian, Dutch and Danish,
Crossing their veins until they vanish
In one conglomeration!
So subtle a tangle of Blood, indeed,
No heraldry-Harvey will ever succeed
In finding the circulation!

XV.

Depend upon it, my snobbish friend,
Your family thread you can't ascend,
Without good reason to apprehend
You may find it waxed at the farther end
By some plebeian vocation!
Or, worse than that, your boasted Line
May end in a loop of stronger twine,
That plagued some worthy relation!

XVI.

But Miss Mac Bride hath something beside
Her lofty birth to nourish her pride. —

For rich was the old paternal Mac Bride,
    According to public rumor;
And he lived 'Up Town,' in a splendid Square,
And kept his daughter on dainty fare,
And gave her gems that were rich and rare,
And the finest rings and things to wear,
    And feathers enough to plume her!

XVII.

An honest mechanic was John Mac Bride,
As ever an honest calling plied,
    Or graced an honest ditty;
For John had worked in his early day,
In 'Pots and Pearls,' the legends say,
And kept a shop with a rich array
Of things in the soap and candle way,
    In the lower part of the city.

XVIII.

No *rara avis* was honest John,
(That's the Latin for 'sable swan,')
    Though, in one of his fancy flashes,
A wicked wag, who meant to deride,
Called honest John 'Old *Phœnix* Mac Bride,'
    'Because he rose from his ashes!'

XIX.

Little by little he grew to be rich,
By saving of candle-ends and 'sich,'
Till he reached, at last, an opulent niche, —
    No very uncommon affair;

For history quite confirms the law
Expressed in the ancient Scottish saw,
  A MICKLE may come to be May'r! *

XX.

Alack! for many ambitious beaux!
She hung their hopes upon her nose,
  (The figure is quite Horatian! †)
Until from habit the member grew
As queer a thing as ever you knew
  Turn up to observation!

XXI.

A thriving tailor begged her hand,
But she gave 'the fellow' to understand,
  By a violent manual action,
She perfectly scorned the best of his clan,
And reckoned the ninth of any man
  An exceedingly Vulgar Fraction!

XXII.

Another, whose sign was a golden boot,
Was mortified with a bootless suit,
  In a way that was quite appalling;
For though a regular *sutor* by trade,
He was n't a suitor to suit the maid,
Who cut him off with a saw, — and bade
  'The cobbler keep to his calling.'

* Mickle wi' thrift may chance to be mair. — *Scotch Proverb.* Andrew Mickle, former Mayor of New York.

† "Omnia suspendens naso."

XXIII.

(The Muse must let a secret out, —
There is n't the faintest shadow of doubt,
That folks who oftenest sneer and flout
At 'the dirty, low mechanicals,'
Are they whose sires, by pounding their knees,
Or coiling their legs, or trades like these,
Contrived to win their children ease
From poverty's galling manacles.)

XXIV.

A rich tobacconist comes and sues,
And, thinking the lady would scarce refuse
A man of his wealth and liberal views,
Began, at once, with 'If you choose, —
And could you really love him —'
But the lady spoiled his speech in a huff,
With an answer rough and ready enough,
To let him know she was up to snuff,
And altogether above him!

XXV.

A young attorney of winning grace,
Was scarce allowed to 'open his face,'
Ere Miss Mac Bride had closed his case
With true judicial celerity;
For the lawyer was poor, and 'seedy' to boot,
And to say the lady discarded his *suit*,
Is merely a double verity.

XXVI.

The last of those who came to court
Was a lively beau of the dapper sort,
'Without any visible means of support,'—
A crime by no means flagrant
In one who wears an elegant coat,
But the very point on which they vote
A ragged fellow 'a vagrant.'

XXVII.

A courtly fellow was Dapper Jim,
Sleek and supple, and tall and trim,
And smooth of tongue as neat of limb;
And, maugre his meagre pocket,
You'd say, from the glittering tales he told,
That Jim had slept in a cradle of gold,
With Fortunatus to rock it!

XXVIII.

Now Dapper Jim his courtship plied,
(I wish the fact could be denied,)
With an eye to the purse of the old Mac Bride,
And really 'nothing shorter'!
For he said to himself, in his greedy lust,
'Whenever he dies,—as die he must,—
And yields to Heaven his vital trust,
He's very sure to "come down with his dust,"
In behalf of his only daughter.'

XXIX.

And the very magnificent Miss Mac Bride,
Half in love and half in pride,

Quite graciously relented;
And tossing her head, and turning her back,
No token of proper pride to lack,
To be a Bride without the 'Mac,
With much disdain, consented!

XXX.

Alas! that people who 've got their box
Of cash beneath the best of locks,
Secure from all financial shocks,
Should stock their fancy with fancy stocks,
And madly rush upon Wall-street rocks,
Without the least apology!
Alas! that people whose money affairs
Are sound beyond all need of repairs,
Should ever tempt the bulls and bears
Of Mammon's fierce Zoölogy!

XXXI.

Old John Mac Bride, one fatal day,
Became the unresisting prey
Of Fortune's undertakers;
And staking his all on a single die,
His foundered bark went high and dry
Among the brokers and breakers!

XXXII.

At his trade again in the very shop
Where, years before, he let it drop,
He follows his ancient calling,—
Cheerily, too, in poverty's spite,

And sleeping quite as sound at night,
As when, at Fortune's giddy height,
He used to wake with a dizzy fright
From a dismal dream of falling.

XXXIII.

But alas for the haughty Miss Mac Bride!
'T was such a shock to her precious pride!
She could n't recover, although she tried
Her jaded spirits to rally;
'T was a dreadful change in human affairs
From a Place 'Up Town,' to a nook 'Up Stairs,
From an Avenue down to an Alley!

XXXIV.

'T was little condolence she had, God wot,
From her 'troops of friends,' who had n't forgot
The airs she used to borrow;
They had civil phrases enough, but yet
'T was plain to see that their 'deepest regret
Was a different thing from Sorrow!

XXXV.

They owned it could n't have well been worse,
To go from a full to an empty purse;
To expect a reversion and get a 'reverse,'
Was truly a dismal feature;
But it was n't strange, — they whispered, — at all;
That the Summer of pride should have its Fall,
Was quite according to Nature!

XXXVI.

And one of those chaps who make a pun, —
As if it were quite legitimate fun
To be blazing away at every one,
With a regular double-loaded gun, —
 Remarked that moral transgression
Always brings retributive stings
To candle-makers, as well as kings:
And making light of cereous things,
 Was a very wick-ed profession!

XXXVII.

And vulgar people, the saucy churls,
Inquired about 'the price of Pearls,'
 And mocked at her situation;
'She was n't ruined, — they ventured to hope, —
Because she was poor, she need n't mope, —
Few people were better off for soap,
 And that was a consolation!'

XXXVIII.

And to make her cup of woe run over,
Her elegant, ardent, plighted lover
 Was the very first to forsake her;
'He quite regretted the step, 't was true, —
The lady had pride enough "for two,"
But that alone would never do
 To quiet the butcher and baker!

XXXIX.

And now the unhappy Miss Mac Bride,
The merest ghost of her early pride,
Bewails her lonely position;
Cramped in the very narrowest niche,
Above the poor, and below the rich,
Was ever a worse condition?

MORAL.

Because you flourish in worldly affairs,
Don't be haughty, and put on airs,
With insolent pride of station!
Don't be proud, and turn up your nose
At poorer people in plainer clo'es,
But learn, for the sake of your soul's repose,
That wealth 's a bubble, that comes — and goes!
And that all Proud Flesh, wherever it grows,
Is subject to irritation!

THE BRIEFLESS BARRISTER.

A BALLAD.

AN Attorney was taking a turn,
  In shabby habiliments drest;
His coat it was shockingly worn,
  And the rust had invested his vest.

His breeches had suffered a breach,
  His linen and worsted were worse;
He had scarce a whole crown in his hat,
  And not half-a-crown in his purse.

And thus as he wandered along,
  A cheerless and comfortless elf,
He sought for relief in a song,
  Or complainingly talked to himself:—

'Unfortunate man that I am!
  I've never a client but grief:
The case is, I've no case at all,
  And in brief, I've ne'er had a brief!

'I've waited and waited in vain,
  Expecting an "opening" to find,
Where an honest young lawyer might gain
  Some reward for toil of his mind.

''T is not that I'm wanting in law,
  Or lack an intelligent face,
That others have cases to plead,
  While I have to plead for a case.

'O, how can a modest young man
  E'er hope for the smallest progression, —
The profession's already so full
  Of lawyers so full of profession!'

While thus he was strolling around,
  His eye accidentally fell
On a very deep hole in the ground,
  And he sighed to himself, 'It is well!'

To curb his emotions, he sat
  On the curbstone the space of a minute,
Then cried, 'Here's an opening at last!'
  And in less than a jiffy was in it!

Next morning twelve citizens came,
  ('T was the coroner bade them attend,)
To the end that it might be determined
  How the man had determined his end!

'The man was a lawyer, I hear,'
  Quoth the foreman who sat on the corse.
'A lawyer? Alas!' said another,
  'Undoubtedly died of remorse!'

A third said, 'He knew the deceased,
  An attorney well versed in the laws,
And as to the cause of his death,
  'T was no doubt for the want of a cause.'

The jury decided at length,
  After solemnly weighing the matter,
That the lawyer was drown*d*ed, because
  He could not keep his head above water!'

RHYME OF THE RAIL.

SINGING through the forests,
  Rattling over ridges,
Shooting under arches,
  Rumbling over bridges,
Whizzing through the mountains,
  Buzzing o'er the vale,—
Bless me! this is pleasant,
  Riding on the Rail!

Men of different 'stations'
  In the eye of Fame
Here are very quickly
  Coming to the same.
High and lowly people,
  Birds of every feather,
On a common level
  Travelling together!

Gentleman in shorts,
  Looming very tall;
Gentleman at large,
  Talking very small;
Gentleman in tights,
  With a loose-ish mien;
Gentleman in gray,
  Looking rather green.

Gentleman quite old,
  Asking for the news;
Gentleman in black,
  In a fit of blues;
Gentleman in claret,
  Sober as a vicar;
Gentleman in Tweed,
  Dreadfully in liquor!

Stranger on the right,
  Looking very sunny,
Obviously reading
  Something rather funny.
Now the smiles are thicker,
  Wonder what they mean?
Faith, he 's got the KNICKER-
  BOCKER Magazine!

Stranger on the left,
  Closing up his peepers;
Now he snores amain,
  Like the Seven Sleepers;
At his feet a volume
  Gives the explanation,
How the man grew stupid
  From 'Association'!

Ancient maiden lady
  Anxiously remarks,
That there must be peril
  'Mong so many sparks;

Roguish-looking fellow,
  Turning to the stranger,
Says it 's his opinion
  She is out of danger!

Woman with her baby,
  Sitting vis-a-vis;
Baby keeps a squalling,
  Woman looks at me;
Asks about the distance,
  Says it 's tiresome talking,
Noises of the cars
  Are so very shocking!

Market-woman careful
  Of the precious casket,
Knowing eggs are eggs,
  Tightly holds her basket;
Feeling that a smash,
  If it came, would surely
Send her eggs to pot
  Rather prematurely!

Singing through the forests,
  Rattling over ridges,
Shooting under arches,
  Rumbling over bridges,
Whizzing through the mountains,
  Buzzing o'er the vale;
Bless me! this is pleasant,
  Riding on the Rail!

THE RAPE OF THE LOCK;

OR, CAPTAIN JONES'S MISADVENTURE.

I.

To follow the line of Captain Jones
Back to the old ancestral bones
Were surely an idle endeavor;
For all that is known of the family feats
Is that his sire, as a paver of streets,
Had paved his way in a manner that meets
The appellation of clever.

II.

'T were pleasant enough more fully to trace
The various steps in the Captain's race,
If the records of heraldry had 'em;
But History leaps at a single span
From the primitive pair to the pavior-man,
From Adam down to Mac Adam.

III.

'T was rumored indeed, but nobody knows
What credit to give to such rumors as those,
His grandpapa was a cooper;

But getting fatigued with this roundabout mode
Of staving through life, he took to the Road,
As a kind of irregular trooper.

IV.

But soon, although a fellow of pluck,
By a singular turn in the wheel of luck,
He met with a mortal miscarriage,
By means of a cord that was dangling loose,
And fell over his head in a dangerous noose
That was n't at all like Marriage.

V.

A tale invented by foes, no doubt,
Which idle people had helped about,
Till it went alone, it got so stout;
For as to the truth of the story,
I scarcely ought to have named it here,
It seems to me so exceedingly clear,
The fable is Newgate-ory.

VI.

And that 's the pith of the pedigree
Of Captain JONES, whose family tree
Was a little shrub, 't is plain to see;
But what the topers mention
Respecting wine, is true of blood:
It 'needs no bush if it 's only good,'
Much less a tree of the oldest wood,
To warrant the world's attention.

VII.

Now Captain JONES was a five-feet ten,
(The height of CHESTERFIELD'S gentlemen,)
With a manly breadth of shoulder;
And Captain JONES was straight and trim,
With nothing about him anywise slim,
And had for a leg as perfect a limb
As ever astonished beholder!

VIII.

With a calf of such a notable size,
'T would surely have taken the highest prize
At any fair Fair in creation;
'T was just the leg for a prince to sport
Who wished to stand at a Royal Court,
At the head of Foreign Leg-ation!

IX.

And Captain JONES had an elegant foot,
'T was just the thing for his patent boot,
And could so prettily shove it,
'T was a genuine pleasure to see it repeat
In the public walks the Milonian feat
Of bearing the calf above it!

X.

But the Captain's prominent personal charm
Was neither his foot, nor leg, nor arm,
Nor his very *distingue* air;
Nor was it, although you 're thinking upon 't,
The front of his head, but his head and front
Of beautiful coal-black hair!

XI.

So very bright was the gloss they had,
'T would have made a rival raving mad
To look at his raven curls;
Wherever he went, the Captain's hair
Was certain to fix the public stare,
And the constant cry was, 'I declare!'
And 'Did you ever!' and 'Just look there!'
Among the dazzled girls.

XII.

Now Captain JONES was a master bold
Of a merchant-ship some dozen years old,
And every name could have easily told,
(And never confound the 'hull' and the 'hold,')
Throughout her inventory;
And he had travelled in foreign parts,
And learned a number of foreign arts,
And played the deuce with foreign hearts,
As the Captain told the story.

XIII.

He had learned to chatter the French and Spanish,
To splutter the Dutch, and mutter the Danish,
In a way that sounded oracular;
Had gabbled among the Portuguese,
And caught the Tartar, or rather a piece
Of 'broken China,' it was n't Chinese,
Any more than his own vernacular!

XIV.

How Captain Jones was wont to shine
In the line of ships! (not Ships of the Line,)
How he 'd brag of the water over his wine,
And of woman over the water!
And then, if you credit the Captain's phrase,
He was more expert in such queer ways
As 'doubling capes' and 'putting in stays,'
Than any milliner's daughter!

XV.

Now the Captain kept in constant pay
A single Mate, as a Captain may
(In a nautical, not in a naughty way,
As 'mates' are sometimes carried);
But to hear him prose of the squalls that arose
In the dead of the night to break his repose,
Of white-caps and cradles, and such things as those,
And of breezes that ended in regular blows,
You 'd have sworn the Captain was married

XVI.

The Captain's morals were fair enough,
Though a sailor's life is rather rough,
By dint of the ocean's force;
And that one who makes so many, in ships,
Should make, upon shore, occasional 'trips,'
Seems quite a matter of course.

XVII.

And Captain Jones was stiff as a post
To the vulgar fry, but among the most

Genteel and polished, ruled the roast,
As no professional cook could boast
That ever you set your eye on;
Indeed, 't was enough to make him vain,
For the pretty and proud confessed his reign,
And Captain JONES, in manners and mane,
Was deemed a genuine lion.

XVIII.

And the Captain revelled early and late,
At the balls and routs of the rich and great,
And seemed the veriest child of *fêtes*,
Though merely a minion of pleasure;
And he laughed with the girls in merry sport,
And paid the mammas the civilest court,
And drank their wine, whatever the sort,
By the nautical rule of 'Any port ——'
You may add the rest at leisure.

XIX.

Miss SUSAN BROWN was a dashing girl
As ever revolved in the waltz's whirl,
Or twinkled a foot in the polka's twirl,
By the glare of spermaceti;
And SUSAN'S form was trim and slight,
And her beautiful skin, as if in spite
Of her dingy name, was exceedingly white,
And her azure eyes were 'sparkling and bright,'
And so was her favorite ditty.

XX.

And SUSAN BROWN had a score of names,
Like the very voluminous Mr. JAMES
(Who got at the Font his strongest claims
To be reckoned a Man of Letters);
But thinking the task will hardly please
Scholars who 've taken the higher degrees,
To be set repeating their A, B, C's,
I choose to reject such fetters as these,
Though merely Nominal fetters.

XXI.

The patronymical name of the maid
Was so completely overlaid
With a long prænominal cover,
That if each additional proper noun
Was laid with additional emphasis down,
Miss SUSAN was done uncommonly BROWN,
The moment her christ'ning was over!

XXII.

And SUSAN was versed in modern romance,
In the Modes of MURRAY and Modes of France,
And had learned to sing and learned to dance,
In a style decidedly pretty;
And SUSAN was versed in classical lore,
In the works of HORACE, and several more
Whose *opera* now would be voted a bore
By the lovers of DONIZETTI.

XXIII.

And SUSAN was rich. Her provident sire
Had piled the dollars up higher and higher,
By dint of his personal labors,
Till he reckoned at last a sufficient amount
To be counted, himself, a man of account
Among his affluent neighbors.

XXIV.

By force of careful culture alone,
Old BROWN'S estate had rapidly grown
A plum for his only daughter;
And, after all the fanciful dreams
Of golden fountains and golden streams,
The sweat of patient labor seems
The true Pactolian water.

XXV.

And while your theorist worries his mind
In hopes 'the magical stone' to find,
By some alchemical gammon,
Practical people, by regular knocks,
Are filling their 'pockets full of rocks'
From the golden mountain of Mammon!

XXVI.

With charms like these, you may well suppose
Miss SUSAN BROWN had plenty of beaux,
Breathing nothing but passion;

And twenty sought her hand to gain,
And twenty sought her hand in vain,
Were 'cut,' and did n't 'come again,'
In the Ordinary fashion.

XXVII.

Captain JONES, by the common voice,
At length was voted the man of her choice,
And she his favorite fair;
It was n't the Captain's manly face,
His native sense, nor foreign grace,
That took her heart from its proper place
And put it into a tenderer case,
But his beautiful coal-black hair!

XXVIII.

How it is, *why* it is, none can tell,
But all philosophers know full well,
Though puzzled about the action,
That of all the forces under the sun
You can hardly find a stronger one
Than capillary attraction.

XXIX.

The locks of canals are strong as rocks;
And wedlock is strong as a banker's box;
And there 's strength in the locks a Cockney cocks
At innocent birds, to give himself knocks;
In the locks of safes, and those safety-locks
They call the Permutation;

But of all the locks that ever were made
In Nature's shops, or the shops of trade,
    The subtlest combination
Of beauty and strength is found in those
Which grace the heads of belles and beaux
    In every civilized nation!

XXX.

The gossips whispered it through the town,
That 'Captain JONES loved SUSAN BROWN;
    But, speaking with due precision,
The gossips' tattle was out of joint,
For the lady's 'blunt' was the only point
    That dazzled the lover's vision!

XXXI.

And the Captain begged, in his smoothest tones,
Miss SUSAN BROWN to be Mistress JONES,—
Flesh of his flesh and bone of his bones,
    Till death the union should sever;
For these are the words employed, of course,
Though Death is cheated, sometimes, by Divorce,
A fact which gives an equivocal force
    To that beautiful phrase, 'forever!'

XXXII.

And SUSAN sighed the conventional 'Nay'
In such a bewitching, affirmative way,
The Captain perceived 't was the feminine 'Ay,'
    And sealed it in such commotion,

That no 'lip-service' that ever was paid
To the ear of a god, or the cheek of a maid,
    Looked more like real devotion!

XXXIII.

And SUSAN'S Mamma made an elegant *fête*
And exhibited all the family plate
    In honor of SUSAN'S lover;
For now 't was settled, another trip
Over the sea in his merchant-ship,
    And his bachelor-ship was over.

XXXIV.

There was an Alderman, well to do,
Who was fond of talking about *vertù*,
And had, besides, the genuine *goût*,
    If one might credit his telling;
And the boast was true beyond a doubt
If he had only pronounced it 'gout,'
    According to English spelling!

XXXV.

A crockery-merchant of great parade,
Always boasting of having made
His large estate in the China trade;
    Several affluent tanners;
A lawyer, whose most important 'case'
Was that which kept his books in place;
His wife, a lady of matchless grace,
Who bought her form, and made her face,
    Who plainly borrowed her manners;

XXXVI

A druggist; an undevout divine;
A banker, who 'd got as rich as a mine
'In the cotton trade and sugar line,'
Along the Atlantic border;
A doctor, fumbling his golden seals;
And an undertaker close at his heels,
Quite in the natural order!

XXXVII.

People of rank, and people of wealth,
Plethoric people in delicate health,
(Who fast in public, and feast by stealth,)
And people slender and hearty,
Flocked in so fast, 't was plain to the eye
Of any observer standing by,
That party-spirit was running high,
And this was the popular party!

XXXVIII.

To tell what griefs and woes betide
The hapless world, from female pride,
Were a long and dismal story;
Alas for SUSAN and womankind!
A sudden ambition seized her mind,
In the height of her party-glory.

XXXIX.

To pique a group of laughing girls
Who stood admiring the Captain's curls,
She formed the resolution

To get a lock of her lover's hair,
In the gaze of the guests assembled there,
By some expedient, foul or fair
Before the party's conclusion.

XL.

'Only a lock, dear Captain! — no more,
"A lock for memory," I implore!'
But JONES, the gayest of quizzers,
Replied, as he gave his eye a cock,
''T is a treacherous memory needs a lock,'
And dodged the envious scissors.

XLI.

Alas that SUSAN could n't refrain,
In her zeal the precious lock to gain,
From laying her hand on the lion's mane!
To see the cruel mocking,
And hear the short, affected cough,
The general titter, and chuckle, and scoff,
When the Captain's Patent Wig came off,
Was really dreadfully shocking!

XLII.

Of SUSAN'S swoon, the tale is told,
That long before her earthly mould
Regained its ghostly tenant,
Her luckless, wigless, loveless lover
Was on the sea, and 'half-seas-over,'
Dreaming that some piratical rover
Had carried away his Pennant!

A RHYMED EPISTLE

TO THE EDITOR OF THE KNICKERBOCKER MAGAZINE.

DEAR KNICK: While myself and my spouse
  Sat tea-ing last evening, and chatting,
And, mindful of conjugal vows,
  Were nicely agreed in combating,
It chanced that myself and my wife,
  ('T was Madam occasioned the pother!)
Falling suddenly into a strife,
  Came near falling out with each other!

In a brisk, miscellaneous chat,
  Quite in tune with the chime of the tea-things,
We were talking of this and of that,
  Just as each of us happened to see things,
When some how or other it chanced,
  (I don't quite remember the cue,)
That as talking and tea-ing advanced,
  We found we were talking of you!

I think — but perhaps I am wrong,
  Such a subtle old chap is Suggestion,
As he forces each topic along
  By the trick of the 'previous question' —

Some remarks on a bacchanal revel
  Suggested that horrible elf
With the hoof and the horns, — and the Devil,
  Excuse me, suggested yourself!

'Ah! Knick, to be sure; by the way,'
  Quoth Madam, 'what sort of a man
Do you take him to be! — nay, but stay,
  And let *me* guess him out if I can.
He 's young, and quite handsome, no doubt;
  Rather slender, and not over-tall;
And he loves a snug little turn-out,
  And turns out "quite a love" at a ball!'

And then she went on to portray
  Such a very delightful ideal,
That a sensible stranger would say
  It really could n't be real.
'And his wife, what a lady must *she* be?
  (Knick's married, that *I* know, and *you* know;)
You 'll find her a delicate Hebe,
  And not your magnificent Juno!'

Now I am a man, you must learn,
  Less famous for beauty than strength,
And, for aught I could ever discern,
  Of rather superfluous length.
In truth 't is but seldom one meets
  Such a Titan in human abodes,
And when I stalk over the streets,
  I 'm a perfect Colossus of roads!

So I frowned like a tragedy-Roman,
  For in painting the beautiful elf
As the form of your lady, the woman
  Took care to be drawing herself;
While, mark you, the picture she drew
  So deused *con amore* and free,
That fanciful likeness of you,
  Was by no means a portrait of me!

'How lucky for ladies,' I hinted,
  'That in our republican land
They may prattle, without being stinted,
  Of matters they don't understand;
I'll show you, dear Madam, that "KNICK"
  Is n't dapper nor daintily slim,
But a gentleman decently thick,
  With a manly extension of limb.

'And as to his youth — talk of flowers
  Blooming gayly in frosty December!
I'll warrant, his juvenile hours
  Are things he can scarcely remember!
Here, Madam, quite plain to be seen,
  Is the chap you would choose for a lover
And, producing your own Magazine,
  I pointed elate to the cover!

'You see, ma'am, 't is just as I said,
  His locks are as gray as a rat;
Here, look at the crown of his head,
  'T is bald as the crown of my hat!

'Nay, my dear,' interrupted my wife,
  Who began to be casting about
To get the last word in the strife,
  ''T is his grandfather's picture, no doubt!'

THE DOG-DAYS.

"Hot! hot! — all piping hot." — *City Cries.*

HEAVEN help us all in these terrific days!
  The burning sun upon the earth is pelting
With his directest, fiercest, hottest rays,
  And everything is melting!

Fat men, infatuate, fan the stagnant air,
  In rash essay to cool their inward glowing,
While with each stroke, in dolorous despair,
  They feel the fever growing!

The lean and lathy find a fate as hard,
  For, all a-dry, they burn like any tinder
Beneath the solar blaze, till withered, charred,
  And crisped away to cinder!

E'en Stoics now are in the melting mood,
  And vestal cheeks are most unseemly florid;
The very zone that girts the frigid prude
  Is now intensely torrid!

The dogs lie lolling in the deepest shade;
  The pigs are all a-wallow in the gutters,
And not a household creature — cat or maid,
  But querulously mutters!

''T is dreadful, dreadful hot!' exclaims each one
  Unto his sweating, sweltering, roasting neighbor
Then mops his brow, and sighs, as he had done
  A quite herculean labor!

And friends who pass each other in the town
  Say no good-morrows when they come together,
But only mutter, with a dismal frown,
  'What horrid, horrid weather!'

While prudent mortals curb with strictest care
  All vagrant curs, it seems the queerest puzzle
The Dog-star rages rabid through the air,
  Without the slightest muzzle!

But Jove is wise and equal in his sway,
  Howe'er it seems to clash with human reason,
His fiery dogs will soon have had their day,
  And men shall have a season!

ON A RECENT CLASSIC CONTROVERSY.

AN EPIGRAM.

NAY, marvel not to see these scholars fight,
In brave disdain of certain scath and scar;
'T is but the genuine old Hellenic spite, —
'When Greek meets Greek, then comes the tug of war!'

ANOTHER.

QUOTH David to Daniel, 'Why is it these scholars
Abuse one another whenever they speak?'
Quoth Daniel to David, 'It nat'rally follers
Folks come to hard words if they meddle with Greek!'

THE GHOST-PLAYER.

A BALLAD.

Tom Goodwin was an actor-man,
  Old Drury's pride and boast
In all the light and sprite-ly parts,
  Especially the Ghost.

Now Tom was very fond of drink,
  Of almost every sort,
Comparative and positive,
  From porter up to port.

But grog, like grief, is fatal stuff
  For any man to sup;
For when it fails to pull him down,
  It's sure to blow him up.

And so it fared with ghostly Tom,
  Who day by day was seen
A-swelling, till (as lawyers say)
  He fairly lost his lean.

At length the manager observed
  He 'd better leave his post,
And said, he played the very deuse
  Whene'er he played the Ghost.

'T was only t' other night he saw
  A fellow swing his hat,
And heard him cry, 'By all the gods!
  The Ghost is getting fat!'

'T would never do, the case was plain;
  His eyes he could n't shut;
Ghosts should n't make the people laugh,
  And Tom was quite a *butt.*

Tom's actor friends said ne'er a word
  To cheer his drooping heart;
Though more than one was burning up
  With zeal to 'take his part.'

Tom argued very plausibly;
  He said he did n't doubt
That Hamlet's father drank and grew,
  In years, a little stout.

And so, 't was natural, he said,
  And quite a proper plan,
To have his spirit represent
  A portly sort of man.

'T was all in vain: the manager
  Said he was not in sport,
And, like a gen'ral, bade poor Tom
  Surrender up his *forte.*

He 'd do perhaps in heavy parts,
  Might answer for a monk,
Or porter to the elephant,
  To carry round his trunk;

But in the Ghost his day was past, —
  He 'd never do for that;
A Ghost might just as well be dead
  As plethoric and fat!

Alas! next day poor Tom was found
  As stiff as any post;
For he had lost his character,
  And given up the Ghost!

ON AN ILL-READ LAWYER.

AN EPIGRAM.

An idle attorney besought a brother
For 'something to read — some novel or other,
    That was really fresh and new.'
'Take Chitty!' replied his legal friend,
'There is n't a book that I could lend
    Would prove more "novel" to you!'

A BENEDICT'S APPEAL TO A BACHELOR

"Double! double!" — *Shakespeare.*

I.

DEAR CHARLES, be persuaded to wed, —
  For a sensible fellow like you,
It 's high time to think of a bed,
  And muffins and coffee for two!
So have done with your doubt and delaying, —
  With a sour so adapted to mingle,
No wonder the neighbors are saying
  'Tis singular you should be single!

II.

Don't say that you have n't got time, —
  That business demands your attention, —
There 's not the least reason nor rhyme
  In the wisest excuse you can mention.
Don't tell me about 'other fish,' —
  Your duty is done when you buy 'em, —
And you never will relish the dish,
  Unless you 've a woman to fry 'em!

III.

Don't listen to querulous stories
  By desperate damsels related,
Who sneer at connubial glories,
  Because they 've known couples mismated.
Such people, if they had their pleasure,
  Because silly bargains are made,
Would deem it a rational measure
  To lay an embargo on trade!

IV.

You may dream of poetical fame,
  But your wishes may chance to miscarry, —
The best way of sending one's name
  To posterity, Charles, is to marry!
And here I am willing to own,
  After soberly thinking upon it,
I 'd very much rather be known
  For a beautiful son, than a sonnet!

V.

To Procrastination be deaf, —
  (A homily sent from above,) —
The scoundrel 's not only 'the thief
  Of time,' but of beauty and love!
O delay not one moment to win
  A prize that is truly worth winning, —
Celibacy, Charles, is a sin,
  And sadly prolific of sinning!

VI.

Then pray bid your doubting good-by,
  And dismiss all fantastic alarms, —
I'll be sworn you've a girl in your eye
  'T is your duty to have in your arms!
Some trim little maiden of twenty,
  A beautiful, azure-eyed elf,
With virtues and graces in plenty,
  And no failing but loving yourself!

VII.

Don't search for 'an angel' a minute;
  For granting you win in the sequel,
The deuse, after all, would be in it,
  With a union so very unequal
The angels, it must be confessed,
  In *this* world are rather uncommon;
And allow me, dear Charles, to suggest
  You'll be better content with a woman!

VIII.

I could furnish a bushel of reasons
  For choosing a conjugal mate, —
It agrees with all climates and seasons,
  And gives you a 'double estate'!
To one's parents 't is (gratefully) due, —
  Just think what a terrible thing
'T would have been, sir, for me and for you,
  If *ours* had forgotten the ring!

IX.

Then there 's the economy — clear,
  By poetical algebra shown, —
If your wife has a grief or a fear,
  One half, by the law, is your own!
And as to the joys — by division,
  They 're nearly quadrupled, 't is said,
(Though I never could see the addition
  Quite plain in the item of bread).

X.

Remember, I do not pretend
  There 's anything 'perfect' about it,
But this I 'll aver to the end,
  Life 's very imperfect without it!
'T is not that there 's 'poetry' in it, —
  As, doubtless, there may be to those
Endowed with a genius to win it, —
  But I 'll warrant you excellent prose!

XI.

Then, Charles, be persuaded to wed, —
  For a sensible fellow like you,
It 's high time to think of a bed,
  And muffins and coffee for two;
So have done with your doubt and delaying, —
  With a soul so adapted to mingle,
No wonder the neighbors are saying
  'T is singular you should be single!

BOYS.

'THE proper study of mankind is man,'—
The most perplexing one, no doubt, is woman
The subtlest study that the mind can scan,
Of all deep problems, heavenly or human!

But of all studies in the round of learning,
From nature's marvels down to human toys,
To minds well fitted for acute discerning,
The very queerest one is that of boys!

If to ask questions that would puzzle Plato,
And all the schoolmen of the Middle Age,—
If to make precepts worthy of old Cato,
Be deemed philosophy,—your boy 's a sage!

If the possession of a teeming fancy,
(Although, forsooth, the younker does n't know it,)
Which he can use in rarest necromancy,
Be thought poetical, your boy 's a poet!

If a strong will and most courageous bearing,
If to be cruel as the Roman Nero;
If all that 's chivalrous, and all that 's daring,
Can make a hero, then the boy 's a hero!

But changing soon with his increasing stature,
The boy is lost in manhood's riper age,
And with him goes his former triple nature, —
No longer Poet, Hero, now, nor Sage!

WOMAN'S WILL.

AN EPIGRAM.

Men dying make their wills, — but wives
Escape a work so sad;
Why should they make what all their lives
The gentle dames have had?

THE COLD-WATER MAN.

A BALLAD.

It was an honest fisherman,
  I knew him passing well, —
And he lived by a little pond,
  Within a little dell.

A grave and quiet man was he,
  Who loved his hook and rod, —
So even ran his line of life,
  His neighbors thought it odd.

For science and for books, he said
  He never had a wish, —
No school to him was worth a fig,
  Except a school of fish.

He ne'er aspired to rank or wealth,
  Nor cared about a name, —
For though much famed for fish was he,
  He never fished for fame!

Let others bend their necks at sight
  Of Fashion's gilded wheels,
He ne'er had learned the art to 'bob'
  For anything but eels!

A cunning fisherman was he,
  His angles all were right;
The smallest nibble at his bait
  Was sure to prove 'a bite'!

All day this fisherman would sit
  Upon an ancient log,
And gaze into the water, like
  Some sedentary frog;

With all the seeming innocence,
  And that unconscious look,
That other people often wear
  When they intend to 'hook'!

To charm the fish he never spoke, —
  Although his voice was fine,
He found the most convenient way
  Was just to drop a line!

And many a gudgeon of the pond,
  If they could speak to-day,
Would own, with grief, this angler had
  A mighty taking way!

Alas! one day this fisherman
  Had taken too much grog,
And being but a landsman, too,
  He could n't keep the log!

'T was all in vain with might and main
  He strove to reach the shore;
Down — down he went, to feed the fish
  He 'd baited oft before!

The jury gave their verdict that
  'T was nothing else but gin
Had caused the fisherman to be
  So sadly taken in;

Though one stood out upon a whim,
  And said the angler's slaughter,
To be exact about the fact,
  Was, clearly, gin-and-*water!*

The moral of this mournful tale,
  To all is plain and clear, —
That drinking habits bring a man
  Too often to his bier;

And he who scorns to 'take the pledge,
  And keep the promise fast,
May be, in spite of fate, a *stiff*
  Cold-water man at last!

ON AN UGLY PERSON SITTING FOR A DAGUERROTYPE.

AN EPIGRAM.

HERE Nature in her glass — the wanton elf—
Sits gravely making faces at herself;
And, while she scans each clumsy feature o'er,
Repeats the blunders that she made before!

A COLLEGE REMINISCENCE.

ADDRESSED TO THOMAS B. THORPE, ESQ., OF NEW ORLEANS.

Dear Tom, have you forgot the day
When, long ago, we used to stray
Among the 'Haddams'?
Where, in the mucky road, a man
(The road was built on Adam's plan,
And not McAdam's!)

Went down — down — down, one stormy night,
And disappeared from human sight,
All save his hat, —
Which raised in sober minds a sense
Of some mysterious Providence
In sparing that?

I think 't will please you, Tom, to hear
The man who in that night of fear
Went down terrestrial,
Worked out a passage like a miner,
And, pricking through somewhere in China,
Came up Celestial!

Ah! those were memorable times,
And worth embalming in my rhymes,
When, at the summons
Of chapel bell, we left our sport
For lessons most uncommon short,
Or shorter commons!

I mind me Tom, you often drew
Nice portraits, and exceeding true —
To your intention!
The most impracticable faces
Discovered unsuspected graces,
By your invention.

On brainless heads the finest bumps
(Erected by your pencil-thumps)
Were plainly seen;
Your Yankees all were very Greek,
Unchosen aunts grew 'choice antique,'
And blues turned green!

The swarthy suddenly were fair,
And yellow changed to auburn hair
Or sunny flax;
And people very thin and flat,
Like Aldermen, grew round and fat
On canvas-backs!

I well remember all your art
To make the best of every part, —
I am certain *no* man

Could better coax a wrinkle out,
Or elevate a lowly snout,
Or snub a Roman!

Young gentlemen with leaden eyes
Stared wildly out on lowering skies,
Quite Corsair-fashion;
And greenish orbs got very blue,
And linsey-woolsey maidens grew
Almost Circassian!

And many an ancient maiden aunt
As lean and lank as John O'Gaunt,
Or even lanker,
By art transformed and newly drest,
Could boast for once as full a chest
As — any banker!

Ah! we were jolly youngsters then,
But now we 're sober-sided men,
Half through life's journey;
And you 've turned author, Tom, I hear, —
And I — you 'll think it very queer —
Have turned attorney!

Heaven bless you, Tom, in house and heart!
(That we should live so far apart
Is much a pity,)
And may you multiply your name,
And have a very 'crescent' fame,
Just like your city!

FAMILY QUARRELS.

AN EPIGRAM.

'A FOOL,' said Jeanette, 'is a creature I hate!'
'But hating,' quoth John, 'is immoral;
Besides, my dear girl, it's a terrible fate
To be found in a family quarrel!'

SONNET TO A CLAM.

Dum tacent *clam*ant.

INGLORIOUS FRIEND ! most confident I am
  Thy life is one of very little ease ;
  Albeit men mock thee with their similes
And prate of being ' happy as a clam ' !
What though thy shell protects thy fragile head
  From the sharp bailiffs of the briny sea ?
  Thy valves are, sure, no safety-valves to thee,
While rakes are free to desecrate thy bed,
And bear thee off, — as foemen take their spoil, —
  Far from thy friends and family to roam ;
  Forced, like a Hessian, from thy native home,
To meet destruction in a foreign broil !
  Though thou art tender, yet thy humble bard
  Declares, O clam ! thy case is shocking hard !

A REASONABLE PETITION.

You say, dearest girl, you esteem me,
  And hint of respectful regard,
And I'm certain it would n't beseem me
  Such an excllent gift to discard.
But even the Graces, you 'll own,
  Would lose half their beauty apart,—
And Esteem, when she stands all alone,
  Looks most unbecomingly tart.
So grant me, dear girl, this petition :—
  If Esteem e'er again should come hither,
Just to keep her in cheerful condition,
  Let Love come in company with her !

GUNEOPATHY.

I SAW a lady yesterday,
  A regular M. D.,
Who 'd taken from the Faculty
  Her medical degree;
And I thought, if ever I was sick,
  My doctor she should be!

I pity the deluded man
  Who foolishly consults
Another man, in hopes to find
  Such magical results
As when a pretty woman lays
  Her hand upon his pulse!

I had a strange disorder once,
  A kind of chronic chill,
That all the doctors in the town,
  With all their vaunted skill,
Could never cure, I 'm very sure,
  With powder nor with pill;

I don't know what they called it
  In their pompous terms of Art,

Nor if they thought it mortal
  In such a vital part, —
I only know 't was reckoned
  'Something icy round the heart'!

A lady came, — her presence brought
  The blood into my ears!
She took my hand — and something like
  A fever now appears!
Great Galen! — I was all aglow,
  Though I'd been cold for years!

Perhaps it is n't every case
  That's fairly in her reach,
But should I e'er be ill again,
  I fervently beseech
That I may have, for life or death,
  A lady for my 'leech'!

A PHILOSOPHICAL QUERY.

TO ——.

If Virtue be measured by what we resist,
  When against Inclination we strive,
You and I have been proved, we may fairly insist,
  The most virtuous mortals alive!
Now Virtue, we know, is the brightest of pearls,
  But as Pleasure is hard of evasion,
Should we envy, or pity, the stoical churls
  Who never have known a temptation?

COMIC MISERIES.

I.

My dear young friend, whose shining wit
  Sets all the room ablaze,
Don't think yourself 'a happy dog,'
  For all your merry ways;
But learn to wear a sober phiz,
  Be stupid, if you can,
It 's such a very serious thing
  To be a funny man!

II.

You 're at an evening party, with
  A group of pleasant folks, —
You venture quietly to crack
  The least of little jokes:
A lady does n't catch the point,
  And begs you to explain, —
Alas for one who drops a jest
  And takes it up again!

III.

You 're talking deep philosophy
  With very special force,

To edify a clergyman
  With suitable discourse:
You think you 've got him, — when he calls
  A friend across the way,
And begs you 'll say that funny thing
  You said the other day!

IV.

You drop a pretty *jeu-de-mot*
  Into a neighbor's ears,
Who likes to give you credit for
  The clever thing he hears,
And so he hawks your jest about,
  The old, authentic one,
Just breaking off the point of it,
  And leaving out the pun!

V.

By sudden change in politics,
  Or sadder change in Polly,
You lose your love, or loaves, and fall
  A prey to melancholy,
While everybody marvels why
  Your mirth is under ban, —
They think your very grief 'a joke,'
  You 're such a funny man!

VI.

You follow up a stylish card
  That bids you come and dine,

And bring along your freshest wit
  (To pay for musty wine);
You 're looking very dismal, when
  My lady bounces in,
And wonders what you 're thinking of,
  And why you don't begin!

VII.

You 're telling to a knot of friends
  A fancy-tale of woes
That cloud your matrimonial sky,
  And banish all repose,—
A solemn lady overhears
  The story of your strife,
And tells the town the pleasant news:—
  You quarrel with your wife!

VIII.

My dear young friend, whose shining wit
  Sets all the room ablaze,
Don't think yourself 'a happy dog,'
  For all your merry ways;
But learn to wear a sober phiz,
  Be stupid, if you can,
It 's such a very serious thing
  To be a funny man!

THE OLD CHAPEL-BELL.

A BALLAD.*

WITHIN a churchyard's sacred ground,
  Whose fading tablets tell
Where they who built the village church
  In solemn silence dwell,
Half hidden in the earth, there lies
  An ancient Chapel-Bell.

Broken, decayed, and covered o'er
  With mouldering leaves and rust;
Its very name and date concealed
  Beneath a cankering crust;
Forgotten — like its early friends,
  Who sleep in neighboring dust.

---

* This ballad is a paraphrase of a beautiful prose tale written by Mrs. ALICE B. NEAL, and published anonymously, several years ago, as a translation 'from the German.' The story is so exceedingly *Germanesque* in its style and spirit, that the best scholars in the country did not suspect its American origin, until the fact was recently disclosed by the gifted authoress.

Yet it was once a trusty Bell,
  Of most sonorous lung,
And many a joyous wedding-peal,
  And many a knell had rung,
Ere Time had cracked its brazen sides,
  And broke its iron tongue.

And many a youthful heart had danced,
  In merry Christmas-time,
To hear its pleasant roundelay,
  Sung out in ringing rhyme;
And many a worldly thought been checked
  To list its Sabbath chime.

A youth — a bright and happy boy,
  One sultry summer's day,
Aweary of his bat and ball,
  Chanced hitherward to stray,
To read a little book he had,
  And rest him from his play.

'A soft and shady spot is this!'
  The rosy youngster cried,
And sat him down, beneath a tree,
  That ancient Bell beside;
(But, hidden in the tangled grass,
  The Bell he ne'er espied.)

Anon, a mist fell on his book,
  The letters seemed to stir

And though, full oft, his flagging sight
  The boy essayed to spur,
The mazy page was quickly lost
  Beneath a cloudy blur.

And while he marvelled much at this,
  And wondered how it came,
He felt a languor creeping o'er
  His young and weary frame,
And heard a voice, a gentle voice,
  That plainly spoke his name.

That gentle voice that named his name
  Entranced him like a spell,
Upon his ear so very near
  And suddenly it fell,
Yet soft and musical, as 't were
  The whisper of a bell.

'Since last I spoke,' the voice began,
  'Seems many a dreary year!
(Albeit, 't is only since thy birth
  I 've lain neglected here!)
Pray list, while I rehearse a tale
  Behooves thee much to hear.

'Once, from yon ivied tower, I watched
  The villagers, around,
And gave to all their joys and griefs
  A sympathetic sound,—
But most are sleeping, now, within
  This consecrated ground.

'I used to ring my merriest peal
  To hail the blushing bride;
I sadly tolled for men cut down
  In strength and manly pride;
And solemnly, — not mournfully, —
  When little children died.

'But, chief, my duty was to bid
  The villagers repair,
On each returning Sabbath morn
  Unto the House of Prayer,
And in his own appointed place
  The Saviour's mercy share.

'Ah! well I mind me of a child,
  A gleesome, happy maid,
Who came, with constant step, to church,
  In comely garb arrayed,
And knelt her down full solemnly,
  And penitently prayed.

'And oft, when church was done, I marked
  That little maiden near
This pleasant spot, with book in hand,
  As you are sitting here, —
She read the Story of the Cross,
  And wept with grief sincere.

'Years rolled away, — and I beheld
  The child to woman grown;

Her cheek was fairer, and her eye
With brighter lustre shone;
But childhood's truth and innocence
Were still the maiden's own.

'I never rang a merrier peal
Than when, a joyous bride,
She stood beneath the sacred porch,
A noble youth beside,
And plighted him her maiden troth,
In maiden love and pride.

'I never tolled a deeper knell,
Than when, in after years,
They laid her in the churchyard here,
Where this low mound appears —
(The very grave, my boy, that you
Are watering now with tears !)

'*It is thy mother!* gentle boy,
That claims this tale of mine, —
Thou art a flower whose fatal birth
Destroyed the parent vine!
A precious flower art thou, my child, —
TWO LIVES WERE GIVEN FOR THINE!

'One was thy sainted mother's, when
She gave thee mortal birth;
And one thy Saviour's, when in death
He shook the solid earth;
Go! boy, and live as may befit
Thy life's exceeding worth!'

The boy awoke, as from a dream,
  And, thoughtful, looked around,
But nothing saw, save at his feet
  His mother's lowly mound,
And by its side that ancient Bell,
  Half hidden in the ground!

THE LADY ANN.

A BALLAD.

'SHE 'LL soon be here, the Lady Ann,'
  The children cried in glee;
'She always comes at four o'clock,
  And now it 's striking three.'

At stroke of four the lady came,
  A lady passing fair;
And she sat and gazed adown the road,
  With a long and eager stare.

'The mail! the mail!' the idlers cried,
  At sight of a coach-and-four;
'The mail! the mail!' and at the word,
  The coach was at the door.

Up sprang in haste the Lady Ann,
  And marked with anxious eye
The travellers, who, one by one,
  Were slowly passing by.

'Alack! alack!' the lady cried,
  'He surely named to-day;
He 'll come to-morrow, then,' she sighed,
  And, turning, strolled away.

''T is passing odd, upon my word,'
  The landlord now began;
'A strange romance! — that woman, Sirs,
  Is called the Lady Ann.

'She dwells hard by upon the hill,
  The widow of Sir John,
Who died abroad, come August next,
  Just twenty years agone.

'A hearty neighbor, Sirs, was he,
  A bold, true-hearted man;
And a fonder pair were seldom seen
  Than he and Lady Ann.

'They scarce had been a twelvemonth wed,
  When — ill betide the day! —
Sir John was called to go in haste
  Some hundred miles away.

'Ne'er lovers in the fairy tales
  A truer love could boast;
And many were the gentle words
  That came and went by post.

'A month or more had passed away,
 When by the post came down
The joyous news that such a day
 Sir John would be in town.

'Full gleesome was the Lady Ann
 To read the welcome word,
And promptly at the hour she came,
 To meet her wedded lord.

'Alas! alas! he came not back!
 There only came instead
A mournful message by the post,
 That good Sir John was dead!

'One piercing shriek, and Lady Ann
 Had swooned upon the floor:
Good Sirs, it was a fearful grief
 That gentle lady bore!

'We raised her up; her ebbing life
 Began again to dawn;
She muttered wildly to herself, —
 'T was plain her wits were gone.

'A strange forgetfulness came o er
 Her sad, bewildered mind,
And to the grief that drove her mad
 Her memory was blind!

'Ah! since that hour she little wots
  Full twenty years are fled!
She little wots, poor Lady Ann!
  Her wedded lord is dead.

'But each returning day she deems
  The day he fixed to come;
And ever at the wonted hour
  She 's here to greet him home.

'And when the coach is at the door,
  She marks with eager eye
The travellers, as one by one
  They 're slowly passing by.

'"Alack!" she cries, in plaintive tone,
  "He surely named to-day!
He 'll come to-morrow, then," she sighs,
  And, turning, strolls away.'

GIRLHOOD.

WITH rosy cheeks, and merry-dancing curls,
    And eyes of tender light,
O, very beautiful are little girls,
    And goodly to the sight!

Here comes a group to seek my lonely bower,
    Ere waning Autumn dies: —
How like the dew-drops on a drooping flower,
    Are smiles from gentle eyes!

What beaming gladness lights each fairy face
    The while the elves advance,
Now speeding swiftly in a gleesome race,
    Now whirling in a dance!

What heavenly pleasure o'er the spirit rolls,
    When all the air along
Floats the sweet music of untainted souls,
    In bright, unsullied song!

The sacred nymphs that guard this sylvan ground
May sport unseen with these,
And joy to hear their ringing laugh resound
Among the clustering trees!

With rosy cheeks, and merry-dancing curls,
And eyes of tender light,
O, very beautiful are little girls,
And goodly to the sight!

BEREAVEMENT.

A SONNET.

Nay, weep not, dearest, though the child be dead,
He lives again in Heaven's unclouded life,
With other angels that have early fled
From these dark scenes of sorrow, sin, and strife.
Nay, weep not, dearest, though thy yearning love
Would fondly keep for earth its fairest flowers,
And e'en deny to brighter realms above
The few that deck this dreary world of ours:
Though much it seems a wonder and a woe
That one so loved should be so early lost,
And hallowed tears may unforbidden flow
To mourn the blossom that we cherished most,
Yet all is well; God's good design I see,
That where our treasure is, our hearts may be!

MY BOYHOOD.

Ah me! those joyous days are gone!
I little dreamt, till they were flown,
    How fleeting were the hours!
For lest he break the pleasing spell,
Time bears for youth a muffled bell,
    And hides his face in flowers!

Ah! well I mind me of the days,
Still bright in memory's flattering rays,
    When all was fair and new;
When knaves were only found in books,
And friends were known by friendly looks,
    And love was always true!

While yet of sin I scarcely dreamed,
And everything was what it seemed,
    And all too bright for choice;
When fays were wont to guard my sleep,
And *Crusoe* still could make me weep,
    And *Santa Claus*, rejoice!

When Heaven was pictured to my thought,
(In spite of all my mother taught
    Of happiness serene,)

A theatre of boyish plays, —
One glorious round of holidays,
    Without a school between!

Ah me! those joyous days are gone;
I little dreamt, till they were flown,
    How fleeting were the hours!
For, lest he break the pleasing spell,
Time bears for youth a muffled bell,
    And hides his face in flowers!

THE TIMES.

A POEM READ BEFORE THE BOSTON MERCANTILE LIBRARY ASSOCIATION, NOVEMBER 14, 1849.

THE Muses once, — so sacred myths declare, —
(See classic Keightly, Cruzer, or Lempriere,) —
On cleft Parnassus held a lofty seat,
Where, in the quiet of their calm retreat,
With sweet accord they spent the rosy hours,
And wove bright garlands of perennial flowers;
Nine blooming sisters, each with separate aim,
Yet all rejoicing in the common fame,
Alone attentive to their high behests,
No jealous cares disturbed their tender breasts,
For Phœbus, watchful of the sacred Nine,
Warned off intruders with a magic sign! —
You've seen the like in Lowell mills, where scores,
In gold or ochre, guard the inner doors;
A frequent sight in any factory town,
Where idle cit, or curious country clown,
Reads, at a glance, in letters large and clear,
The startling caution, — 'No admittance here!'
What amorous bard, the hidden Nine to view,
First scaled the wall, or forced a passage through, —

What 'gay Lothario' found at length a way
To win the maids and lead them all astray, —
Is yet unknown: — this only can be told,
Some curst intruder broke Apollo's fold,
And all-remorseless for the grave abuse,
In Phœbus' spite let all the Muses loose!
Far from their old Parnassian groves to roam, —
To grace, instead, some airy garret-home,
(Where, free from bailiffs, poetasters rhyme,
And, thankless, waste their tapers and their time,
While through the night they fondly toil for naught,
Angling in inkstands for some gudgeon-thought).
Nor this the worst that sprang from such a cause.
Released at once from chaste Diana's laws,
All moral canons eager now to waive,
Save only those that wanton Nature gave,
The Nine are grown a thousand! — and the Earth
Hails every morning yet another birth!

What hinders then, when every youth may choose,
As Fancy bids, a musket or a Muse,
And throw his lead among his fellow-men,
From the dark muzzle of a gun or pen;
When blooming school-girls, who absurdly think
That naught but drapery can be spoiled with ink,
Ply ceaseless quills, that, true to early use,
Keep the old habit of the pristine goose,
While each, a special Sappho in her teens,
Shines forth a goddess in the magazines;
When waning spinsters, happy to rehearse
Their maiden griefs in doubly grievous verse,

Write doleful ditties, or distressful strains,
To wicked rivals, or unfaithful swains,
Or serenade, at night's bewitching noon,
The mythic man whose home is in the moon;
When pattern wives no thrifty arts possess,
Save that of weaving — fustian for the Press,
Write Lyrics, heedless of their scorching buns,
Dress up their Sonnets, but neglect their sons,
Make dainty doughnuts from Parnassian wheat,
And fancy-stockings for poetic feet, —
While husbands — those who love their coffee hot,
And like no 'fire' that does n't boil the pot —
Wish old Apollo, just to plague his life,
Had, for his own, a literary wife!
What hinders then that I, a sober elf,
Who, like the others, keep a Muse myself,
Should venture here, as kind occasion lends
A fitting time to please these urgent friends,
To waive at once my modest Muse's doubt,
And, jockey-like, to trot the lady out? —
An honest creature, I am bound to say,
Who does her duty in a roguish way;
A laughing jade, of not ungentle mould,
Although, in sooth, she 's something apt to scold,
And, like some worthy people you have seen,
Who 're always talking sharper than they mean,
A genuine Sphinx as ever poet sung,
With much good-nature and a shrewish tongue!
Yet, like your neighbor, be it understood,
She never censures but for public good,
And like her, too, would feel herself unsexed
If voted angry when she 's only vexed!

Don't let me rouse unreasonable fears,
While I, like Brutus, ask you for your ears;
Bear as you can the transient twinge of pain,
In half an hour you 'll have them back again.

We 're a vast people — that 's beyond a doubt —
And nothing loath to let the secret out!
Vain were his labors who should now begin
To stop our growth, or fence the country in!
Let the bold sceptic who denies our worth
Just hear it proved on any 'Glorious Fourth,'
When patriot tongues the thrilling tale rehearse
In grand orations, or resounding verse;
When poor John Bull beholds his navies sink
Before the blast, in swelling floods of ink,
And vents his wrath till all around is blue,
To see his armies yearly flogged anew;
While honest Dutchmen, round the speaker's stand,
Forget, for once, their dearer father-land,
And thrifty Caledonians bless the fate
That gives them freedom at so cheap a rate,
And a clear right to celebrate the day,
And not a baubee for the boon to pay;
And Gallia's children prudently relieve
Their bursting bosoms, with as loud a 'vive'
For 'L'Amérique,' as when their voices swell
With equal glory for 'la bagatelle;'
And ardent sons of Erin's blessèd Isle
Grow patriotic in the Celtic style,
And, all for friendship, bruise each other's eyes,
As when Saint Patrick claims the sacrifice;

While thronging Yankees, all intent to hear,
As if the speaker were an auctioneer,
Swell with the theme, till every mother's son
Feels all his country's magnitude his own!
  You 'll hear about that sturdy little flock
Who landed once on Plymouth's barren rock,
Daring the dangers of the angry main,
For civil freedom and for godly gain;
An honest, frugal, hardy, dauntless band,
Who sought a refuge in this Western land,
Where — (if their own quaint language I may use
That carried back the first Colonial news) —
'Where all the saints may worship as they wish,
And catch abundance of the finest fish!'
  You 'll hear, amazed, the hardships they endured,
To what untold privations were inured, —
What wondrous feats of stout, herculean toil,
Ere they subdued the savage and the soil,
And drave, at last, the intruding heathen out,
Till Witches, Quakers, all were put to rout!

  Here grant the Muse one moment to explain,
Lest you accuse her of a mocking strain.
I love the Puritan; and from my youth
Was taught to admire his valor and his truth.
The veriest caviller must acknowledge still
His honest purpose, and his manly will.
I own I reverence that peculiar race
Who valued steeples less than Christian grace,
Preferred a hut where frost and freedom reigned,
To sumptuous halls at freedom's cost obtained,

And, proudly scorning all that royal knaves,
For bartered conscience, sold to cringing slaves,
Gave up their homes for rights respected more
Than all the allurements of their native shore,
In stranger lands their tattered flag unfurled,
And taught this doctrine to a startled world:
'Mitres and thrones are man-created things,—
We own no master, save the King of kings!'

'T is little marvel that their honored name
Bears, as it must, some maculæ of shame;
'T is only pity that they e'er forgot
The golden lessons their experience taught;
Thought 'Toleration' due to 'saints alone,
And 'Rights of Conscience' only meant their own,
Enforcing laws, concocted to their need,
On all nonjurors to the ruling creed,
Till Baptists groaned beneath their iron heel,
And Quakers quaked with unaccustomed zeal!

And when I hear, as oft the listener may
In song and sermon on a festal day,
Their virtues lauded to the wondering skies,
As none were e'er so great, or good, or wise,
I straight bethink me of the Irish wit,
(A people famed for many a ready hit,)
Who, sitting once, and rather ill at ease,
To hear, in prose, such huge hyperboles,
Gave for a toast, to chide the fulsome tone,
'Old Plymouth Rock,—the Yankee Blarney-stone!

But to resume, — as other preachers say,
Led by their twentieth episode astray,
And thus recall their pristine theme anew,
Lost in the mazes of the shifting view, —
But to resume: these hardy pioneers
Grow, in the flight of scarce a hundred years,
Till, where a few weak colonies were seen,
Thrive in their strength 'the glorious Old Thirteen;
And these, anon, released from British rule,
Swarm like the pupils of a parish school;
And still they flourish at a wondrous rate,
Towns follow towns, and state succeeds to state,
Until, at last, among its crimson bars,
Our country's banner, crowded full of stars,
O'er Freedom's sons in happy triumph waves,
Some twenty millions, — not to count the slaves!

We 're fond of Missions, and rejoice to lend
Our ready aid the Gospel light to send
To chase the gloom that clouds the Pagan's soul,
And haply make his broken spirit whole;
To take the wanderer led by sin astray,
And win his footsteps to the better way.
No cavilling voice at schemes like this I raise, —
All this is well, and to the nation's praise.
Still let the work with growing force proceed,
That kindly answers to the Heathen's need.
But O that some brave proselyte would come
And preach good morals to the folks at home!
O that the next Australian whom they get
Safe in the meshes of the Gospel net,

Straight to our country may be kindly brought,
With all the Christian doctrine he has got,
That he may teach it, uncorrupt, and clear
Of all perversion, to our Heathen here!
Accursed War, and deadly lust of Gold,
These and their horrors let his eyes behold,
Now, — in the moral summer of the days, —
Here, — in the focus of the Gospel blaze, —
How would he beg the doctors to explain,
And solve the puzzle ere it turned his brain!
And when their best excuses he had heard,
How would his breast with honest zeal be stirred
To teach our graduates in the Christian school
The simple lessons of the Golden Rule!
And how, the while he spoke with pleasure true,
As one unfolding something good and new,
How would the wings of his amazement soar
To find their ears had heard it all before!

O murderous War! how long shall History choose
Thee for the favorite topic of her Muse?
As if the real business of mankind,
The noblest purpose of the immortal mind,
Were shown in him who has the greatest skill
In that old mystery, — the art to kill!
And he adorned with most heroic grace,
Who deals the largest slaughter to the race!

A neighboring people rich in landed spoils,
But weak with ignorance and domestic broils;
A haughty nation, full of pride for what
Their fathers were, although themselves are not;

A people fond of pageants and parade,
Replete at once with gas and gasconade,
With all the vapor of the Spanish sire,
Without a flicker of Castilian fire, —
A race like this — O tell it not in Gath! —
Excites our avarice and provokes our wrath,
And so we loose the fiendish dogs of war,
And ply our stripes to gain another star!

Tell not, ye Rabbies of the Whiggish creed,
Who trim your doctrines to your party's need,
And let your lips with fluent phrases move
To censure measures which your acts approve, —
Tell not, except to credulous marines,
How you abhor our recent warlike scenes,
And don't again repeat that precious joke
Which gives the odium *all* to Colonel Polk,
For he may find, who probes the matter well,
At least a dozen Colonels in the shell!
Pray just review the leaders of the bands,
And, as you pass them, let them raise their hands;
Count well the blades that glitter in the sun,
And mark their gallant bearers, one by one, —
For every Whig whose sword your eye may catch,
You 'll scarcely find a 'Loco-foco' match!
We 're all alike, — no thinking man defines
The people's temper by their party lines.
With bright exceptions, few and far between,
Like spots of verdure in a winter scene,
From Rio Grandé to Penobscot's flood,
The whole vast nation loves the smell of blood!

But wars cost money; and though fond of wars,
We worship Mammon quite as much as Mars,
And so consent the battle to forego,
And wait till Interest justifies the blow.
Meantime, though Mars upon the shelf is laid,
We yet can summon Draco to our aid.
The cockpit 's vulgar; and the pleasant game
Of baiting bears is reckoned much the same;
'The manly Ring' is held improper, too;
The Duel 's wicked, and will never do;
'T is plain to see as any comet's tail,
That war 's immoral on so small a scale!
But Draco 's grave, decorous, and discreet,
And gives diversions in a mode so neat,
'The most fastidious'—in the showman phrase—
Can't be offended with his bloody ways.
For, like the doctors, though he cut and bleed,
He shows a broad diploma for the deed!
As boys expend their zoölogic rage
On annual tigers in a travelling cage,
So, by the strictest pathologic rule,
A monthly hanging keeps the nation cool!

The public right to guard the common weal
From thief and ruffian, naught but maniac zeal
Will e'er deny, while every worthy cause
Rests in the proper sanction of the laws.
But when will men the Christian lesson learn,
That 't is not theirs to throttle or to burn
Their brother sinner to his mortal hurt,
Only because they deem it his desert?

If no stern need, with loud imperious call,
Demand the forfeit, be it great or small,
Let not your heart usurp the sacred throne
Of Him who said that vengeance was his own!
In meek submission drop the uplifted rod,
And leave the sinner to the sinner's God

In vain we boast the freedom Nature gave:
Alas! the Ethiop 's not the only slave!
When from their chains shall Saxon minds be freed,
The slaves to lust, to party, and to creed?

Slaves to their Clique, who favor or oppose,
As crafty leaders pull the party-nose;
While the 'dear country,' as the reader learns,[8]
Is saved or ruined in quadrennial turns!

Slaves to the Mode, who pinch the aching waist,
And mend God's image to the Gallic taste;
Who sell their comfort for a narrow boot,
Nor heed the 'corn-laws' of the suffering foot!

Slaves to the ruling Sentiment, whose choice
Is but the echo of the public voice,
While their own thoughts the wretches fear to speak,[9]
Not Sundays only, but throughout the week!

Slaves to Antiquity, who put their trust
In mouldy dogmas, mummies, moth, and rust;
Who buy old nothings at the highest cost,
And deem no art worth having till it 's lost!

Slaves to their Sect, who deem all heavenly light
Through one small taper cheers the moral night,—

Which, should it fail to throw its radiant spark,
Would leave the hapless nations in the dark!

Slaves to Consistency and prudent fears,
As if mistakes grew sacred with their years!
Fearful of change, and much ashamed to show
They 're wiser now than twenty years ago,
Because, forsooth, 't would make the matter plain
They once were wrong, and may be so again!

Slaves to Ambition and the lust of fame,
Who sell their substance for a shadowy name,
And barter happy years for one brief hour
Of courtly dalliance with the harlot, Power!

Bond slaves to Avarice, who perversely soil
Their willing hands with hard, unceasing toil,
For no reward except the menial strife,
As knaves turn tread-mills in a convict life!

But lest the Muse should give her hearers pain
By overstraining her heroic strain, —
A metre strong and well contrived, in sooth,
To bear full measures of satiric truth,
But rather grave, and something apt to tire
Those ears perverse that love an easy lyre, —
She 'll drop the proud heroic for a while
For a new topic and a nimbler style,
And, just for change, endeavor to unfold
The shining treasures of the Land of Gold!

EL DORADO.

I.

Hurrah for the land where the moor and the moun-
tain
Are sparkling with treasures no language hath told,
Where the wave of the river and spray of the foun-
tain
Are bright with the glitter of genuine gold!
Who cares for the pleasures and duties of home,
And all the refinements that grow in its bowers?
To the happy Dorado away we will roam, —
'T will be time to 'refine' when the metal is ours!

II.

Hurrah for the country where Mercury and Mam-
mon
Are the rulers enthroned in the Capitol-seat;
Where Order is chaos, and Justice is gammon,
And yet there 's no Bacon to read or to eat!
Let Famine stalk gaunt and ungainly around,
So thin that his features you scarce can behold, —
Who 'd live upon bread at an ounce for a pound?
Or exchange for potatoes his carats of gold?

III.

Hurrah for the country where Ceres and Hymen
Are driven abashed from the bountiful soil,
And Music 's unheard, save the musical chiming
Of pickaxe and pan in the clatter of toil.

Who cares for your dull academical lore ?
  Or would seek for a single philosopher's stone,
When out of the heaps of auriferous ore
  He can fill up his pockets with 'rocks' of his own ?

IV.

Hurrah for the country where Plutus is chief,
  And where, for a wonder especially odd,
His worshippers freely avow their belief,
  And are never ashamed to acknowledge their
    god !
Where the currency 's ruled by a natural law,
  And Biddles and Barings are voted no thanks, —
Where, in spite of the heavy, perpetual draw,
  There 's always abundance of gold in the Banks !

V.

If a brother, seduced by our precious estate,
  And mad with the frenzy that lucre inspires,
Should hit us, some day, on the back of the pate,
  With a heartier thump than affection requires,
And our bodies be hid in the glittering dust, —
  What matters the incident ? why should we care ?
To die very rich is the national lust,
  To be 'buried in gold' is the popular prayer !

VI.

Then away with all doubting and fanciful ills,
  Away with impressions that duty would print,
The Pactolian drops that affection distils
  Can never be coined into drops of the mint !

So hurrah for the land where the moor and the mountain
Are sparkling with treasures no tongue can unfold,
Where the wave of the river and spray of the fountain
Are bright with the glitter of genuine gold!

Let others, dazzled by the shining ore,
Delve in the dirt to gather golden store.
Let others, patient of the menial toil
And daily suffering, seek the precious spoil;
While most shall struggle through the weary years
With naught of Midas save his ample ears!
No hero I, in such a cause to brave
Hunger and pain, the robber and the grave.
I'll work, instead, exempt from hate and harm,
The fruitful 'placers' of my mountain-farm,
Where the bright ploughshare opens richest veins,
From whence shall issue countless golden grains,
Which in the fulness of the year shall come,
In bounteous sheaves, to bless my harvest-home!

But, haply, good may come of mining yet:
'T will help to pay the nation's foreign debt;
'T will further liberal arts; plate rings and pins,
Gild books and coaches, mirrors, signs, and sins;
'T will cheapen pens and pencils, and perchance
May give us honest dealing for Finance,
(That magic art, unknown to darker times
When fraud and falsehood were reputed crimes,

Whose curious laws with nice precision teach
How whole estates are made from parts of speech;
How lying rags for honest coin shall pass,
And foreign gold be paid in native brass!)
'T will save, perhaps, each deep-indebted State
From all temptation to 'repudiate,'
Till Time restore our precious credit lost,
And hush the wail of Peter Plymley's ghost![10]

But lest, O Muse, thy weary friends complain
Thou lov'st o'ermuch the harsh, satiric strain,
Perversely pleased with hateful themes alone,
And ever singing in a scolding tone,
E'en change the note, and dedicate thy lays
For one brief moment to discerning praise.

While drones and dreaming optimists protest,
'The worst is well, and all is for the best;'
And sturdy croakers chant the counter song,
That 'man grows worse, and everything is wrong;
Truth, as of old, still loves a golden mean,
And shuns extremes to walk erect between!
The world improves; with slow, unequal pace,
'The Good Time 's coming' to our hapless race.
The general tide beneath the refluent surge
Rolls on, resistless, to its destined verge!
Unfriendly hills no longer interpose[11]
As stubborn walls to geographic foes,
Nor envious streams run only to divide
The hearts of brethren ranged on either side.
Promethean Science, with untiring eye
Searching the mysteries of the earth and sky;

And cunning Art, with strong and plastic hand
To work the marvels Science may command;
And broad-winged Commerce, swift to carry o'er
Earth's countless blessings to her farthest shore,—
These, and no German nor Genevan sage,
These are the great reformers of the age!
See Art, exultant in her stately car,
On Nature's Titans wage triumphant war!
While e'en the Lightnings by her wondrous skill
Are tamed for heralds of her sovereign will!
Old Ocean's breast a new invader feels,
And heaves in vain to clog her iron wheels;
In vain the Forests marshal all their force,
And Mountains rise to stay her onward course;
From out her path each bold opposer hurled,
She throws her girdle round a captive world!

I 've kept my promise. Of a prosy song
Men want but little, nor that little long;
Yet even dulness may afford relief
On some occasions, if it 's only brief;
As transient cloudlets soothe the aching sight,
Blind with the dazzle of untempered light!
'T is something that my Pegasus, though slow,
Don't stand curvetting when he 's bid to go;
And, clear at least of one egregious fault,
Knows like a Major when and where to halt!
If in his flight he ventured not to soar
Where Helios' son, too rashly, went before,
(A pregnant hint for feeble bards who dare
The awful heights beyond their native air,)

'T was no dull spirit held the nag in check,
But only mercy for his rider's neck, —
Whom, were he lost among the fogs that lie
Between the empyrean and the nether sky,
And headlong hurled to some Bœotian deep,
No pitying nymphs had gathered round to weep![12]

CARMEN LÆTUM:

Recited, after dinner, before the Alumni of Middlebury College, at their Semi-centennial Celebration, August 22, 1850.

A RIGHT loving welcome, my true-hearted Brothers,
Who have come out to visit the kindest of mothers;
You may think as you will, but there is n't a doubt
Alma Mater rejoices, and knows you are out!
Rejoices to see you in gratitude here,
Returning to honor her fiftieth year.
And while the good lady is so overcome
With maternal emotion, she 's stricken quite dumb,
(A thing, I must own, that 's enough to perplex
A shallow observer, who thinks that the sex,
Whatever may be their internal revealings,
Can never be pained with unspeakable feelings,)
Indulge me, dear Brothers, nor think me ill-bred,
If I venture a moment to speak in her stead.
I, who, though the humblest and homeliest one,
Feel the natural pride of a dutiful son,
And esteem it to-day the profoundest of joys,
That, not less than yourselves, I am one of the boys!

First as to her health, which, I'm sorry to say,
Has been better, no doubt, than she finds it to-day;

Yet when you reflect she 's been somewhat neglected,
She 's really as well as could well be expected;
And, spite of ill-treatment and premature fears,
Is a hearty old lady, for one of her years.
Indeed, I must tell you a bit of a tale,
To show you she 's feeling remarkably hale;
How she turned up her nose, but a short time ago,
At a rather good-looking importunate beau,
And how she refused, with a princess-like carriage
'A very respectable offer of marriage.' *

You see, my dear Brothers, a neighboring College
Who values himself on the depth of his knowledge,
With a prayer for her love, and eye to her land
Walked up to the lady and offered his hand.
For a minute or so she was all in a flutter,
And had not a word she could audibly utter;
For she felt in her bosom, beyond all concealing,
A kind of a — sort of a — widow-like feeling!
But recovering soon from the delicate shock,
She held up her head like an old-fashioned clock,
And, with proper composure, went on and defined,
In suitable phrases, the state of her mind;
Said she would n't mind changing her single condition,
Could she fairly expect to improve her position;

* Allusion is had, in this and subsequent lines, to an unsuccessful attempt to unite Middlebury College with the University of Vermont. The affair is here treated with the license of a dinner poem, and with the partiality permitted to the occasion

And thus, by some words of equivocal scope,
Gave her lover decided 'permission to hope.'
It were idle to talk of the billing and cooing
The amorous gentleman used in his wooing;
Or how she replied to his pressing advances,
His *os*cular touches and ocular glances; —
'T is enough that his courtship, by all that is known,
Was quite the old story, and much like your own!

Thus the matter went on, till the lady found out,
One very fine day, what the rogue was about, —
That all that he wanted was merely the power
By marital license to pocket her dower,
And then to discard her in sorrow and shame,
Bereaved of her home and her name and her fame.
In deep indignation she turned on her heel,
With such withering scorn as a lady might feel
For a knave, who, in stealing her miniature case,
Should take the gold setting, and leave her the face!
But soon growing calm as the breast of the deep,
When the breezes are hushed that the waters may sleep,
She sat in her chair, like a dignified elf,
And thus, while I listened, she talked to herself: —
'Nay, 't was idle to think of so foolish a plan
As a match with this pert University-man,
For I have n't a chick but would redden with shame
At the very idea of my losing my name;
And would feel that no sorrow so heavy could come
To his mother, as losing her excellent home.

'T is true I am weak, but my children are strong,
And won't see me suffer privation or wrong;
So, away with the dream of connubial joys,
I 'll stick to the homestead, and look to the boys!'

How joyous, my friends, is the cordial greeting
Which gladdens the heart at a family meeting;
When brothers assemble at Friendship's old shrine,
To look at the present, and talk of 'Lang Syne'!
Ah! well I remember the halcyon years,
Too earnest for laughter, too pleasant for tears,
When life was a boon in yon classical court,
Though lessons were long, and though commons were short!
Ah! well I remember those excellent men,
Professors and tutors, who reigned o'er us then;
Who guided our feet over Science's bogs,
And led us quite safe through Philosophy's fogs.
Ah! well I remember the President's * face,
As he sat at the lecture with dignified grace,
And neatly unfolded the mystical themes
Of various deep metaphysical schemes, —
How he brightened the path of his studious flock,
As he gave them a key to that wonderful *Locke;*
How he taught us to feel it was fatal indeed
With too much reliance to lean upon *Reid;*
That *Stewart* was sounder, but wrong at the last,
From following his master a little too fast, —
Then closed the discourse in a scholarly tone,
With a clear and intelligent creed of his own.

* Joshua Bates, D. D.

That the man had his faults it were safe to infer, —
Though I really don't recollect what they were, —
I barely remember this one little truth,
When his case was discussed by the critical youth,
The Seniors and Freshmen were sure to divide,
And the former were all on the President's side!

And well I remember another, whose praise
Were a suitable theme for more elegant lays;
But even in numbers ungainly and rough,
I must mention the name of our glorious HOUGH!
Who does not remember? for who can forget,
Till Memory's star shall forever have set,
How he sat in his place unaffected and bold,
And taught us more truths than the lesson had told?
Gave a lift to 'Old NOL,' for the love of the right,
And a slap at the Stuarts, with cordial spite;
And, quite in the teeth of conventional rules,
Hurled his adjectives down upon tyrants and fools?
But, chief, he excelled in his proper vocation
Of giving the classics a classic translation;
In Latin and Greek he was almost oracular,
And, what 's more to his praise, understood the vernacular.
O, 't was pleasant to hear him make English of Greek,
Till you felt that no tongue was inherently weak;
While Horace in Latin seemed quite understated,
And rejoiced like old Enoch in being translated!

And others there were — but the hour would fail,
To bring them all up in historic detail;

And yet I would give, ere the moment has fled,
A sigh for the absent, a tear for the dead.
There 's not one of them all, where'er he may rove,
In the shadows of earth, or the glories above,
In the home of his birth, or in lands far away,
But comes back to be kindly remembered to-day!

One little word more, and my duty is done; —
A health to our Mother, from each mother's son!
Unfading in beauty, increasing in strength,
May she flourish in health through the century's
length!
And next when her children come round her to
boast,
May *Esto perpetua* then be the toast!

THE DEVIL OF NAMES.

A LEGEND.

At an old-fashioned inn, with a pendulous sign,
Once graced with the head of the king of the kine,
But innocent now of the slightest 'design,'
Save calling low people to spurious wine, —
While the villagers, drinking and playing 'all fours,
And cracking small jokes, with vociferous roars,
Were talking of horses, and hunting, and — scores
Of similar topics a bar-room adores,
But which rigid morality greatly deplores,
Till as they grew high in their bacchanal revels,
They fell to discoursing of witches and devils, —
A neat single rap,
Just the ghost of a tap,
That would scarcely have wakened a flea from his nap,
Not at all in its sound like your 'Rochester Knocking,'
(Where asses in herds are diurnally flocking,)
But twice as mysterious, and vastly more shocking,
Was heard at the door by the people within,
Who stopped in a moment their clamorous din,

And ceased in a trice from their jokes and their gin ;
When who should appear
But an odd-looking stranger somewhat ' in the sere,'
(He seemed at the least in his sixtieth year,)
And he limped in a manner exceedingly queer,
Wore breeches uncommonly wide in the rear,
And his nose was turned up with a comical sneer,
And he had in his eye a most villanous leer,
Quite enough to make any one tremble with fear!
Whence he came,
And what was his name,
And what his purpose in venturing out,
And whether his lameness was 'gammon' or gout,
Or merely fatigue from strolling about,
Were questions involved in a great deal of doubt, —
When, taking a chair,
With a sociable air,
Like that which your 'Uncle' 's accustomed to wear,
Or a broker determined to sell you a share
In his splended 'New England Gold-mining' affair,
He opened his mouth and went on to declare
That he was a *devil!* — 'The devil you are!'
Cried one of the guests assembled there,
With a sudden start, and a frightened stare!
'Nay, don't be alarmed,' the stranger exclaims,
'At the name of the devil, — *I'm the Devil of Names!*
You 'll wonder why
Such a devil as I,
Who ought, you would say, to be devilish shy,
Should venture in here with never a doubt,
And let the best of his secrets out;

But mind you, my boys,
It's one of the joys
Of the cunningest woman and craftiest man,
To run as quickly as ever they can,
And put a confidant under ban
Not to publish their favorite plan!
And even the de'il
Will sometimes feel
A little of that remarkable zeal,
And (when it's safe) delights to tell
The very deepest *arcana* of — well; —
Besides, my favor this company wins,
For I value next to capital sins
Those out-and-outers who revel in inns!
So, not to delay,
I'm going to say,
In the very fullest and frankest way,
All about my honors and claims,
Projects and plans, and objects and aims,
And *why* I'm called "The Devil of Names!"
I cheat by false graces,
And duplicate faces,
And treacherous praises,
And by hiding bad things under plausible phrases!
I'll give you a sample,
By way of example:
Here's a bottle before me, will suit to a T
For a nice illustration: this liquor, d' ye see,
Is the water of death, though topers agree
To think it, and drink it, as pure "*eau de vie;*"
I know what it is, — that's sufficient for me!

For the blackest of sins, and crimes, and shames,
I find soft words and innocent names.
The Hells devoted to Satan's games
I christen "Saloons" and "Halls," and then,
By another contrivance of mine again,
They 're only haunted by "sporting men," –
A phrase which many a gamester begs,
In spite of the saw that "eggs is eggs,"
To whiten his nigritudinous legs!

'To debauchees I graciously grant
The favor to be "a little gallant,"
And soften vicious vagrancy down,
By civilly speaking of "men about town;"
There 's cheating and lying
In selling and buying,
And all sorts of frauds and dishonest exactions,
I 've brought to the smallest of moral infractions,
Merely by naming them "business transactions!"
There 's swindling, now, is vastly more fine
As "Banking," — a lucky invention of mine,
Worth ten in the *old* diabolical line!

'In lesser matters it's all the same,
I gain the thing by yielding the name;
It 's really quite the broadest of jokes,
But, on my honor, there 's plenty of folks
So uncommonly fond of verbal cloaks,
They can't enjoy the dinners they eat,
Court the "muse of the twinkling feet,"
Laugh or sing, or do anything meet

For Christian people, without a cheat
To make their happiness quite complete!
    The Boston saints
    Are fond of these feints;
A theatre rouses the loudest complaints,
Till it's thoroughly purged from pestilent taints,
By the charm of a name and a pious *Te Deum*, —
Yet they patronize actors, and handsomely fee 'em!
Keep (shade of "the Howards!") a gay "Athenæum,"
And have, above all, a harmless "Museum,"
Where folks who love plays may religiously see 'em!

'But leaving a trifle which cost me more trouble
By far than the worth of so flimsy a bubble,
I come to a matter which really claims
The studious care of the Devil of Names.
There's "Charity" now —'

But the lecture was done,
Like old Goody Morey's, when scarcely begun;
The devil's discourse by its serious teaching
Had set 'em a-snoring, like regular preaching!
One look of disdain on the sleepers he threw,
As in bitter contempt of the slumbering crew,
And the devil had vanished without more ado, —
A trick, I suspect, that he seldom plays you!

PHAËTHON;

OR, THE AMATEUR COACHMAN.

DAN PHAËTHON — so the histories run —
Was a jolly young chap, and a son of the SUN, —
Or rather of PHŒBUS; but as to his mother,
Genealogists make a deuse of a pother,
Some going for one, and some for another!
For myself, I must say, as a careful explorer,
This roaring young blade was the son of AURORA!

Now old Father PHŒBUS, ere railways begun
To elevate funds and depreciate fun,
Drove a very fast coach by the name of 'THE SUN;
Running, they say,
Trips every day,
(On Sundays and all, in a heathenish way,)
All lighted up with a famous array
Of lanterns that shone with a brilliant display,
And dashing along like a gentleman's 'shay,'
With never a fare, and nothing to pay!
Now PHAËTHON begged of his doting old father
To grant him a favor, and this the rather,

Since some one had hinted, the youth to annoy,
That he was n't by any means PHŒBUS'S boy!
Intending, the rascally son of a gun,
To darken the brow of the son of the SUN!
'By the terrible Styx!' said the angry sire,
While his eyes flashed volumes of fury and fire,
'To prove your reviler an infamous liar,
I swear I will grant you whate'er you desire!'
'Then by my head,'
The youngster said,
'I'll mount the coach when the horses are fed! —
For there 's nothing I 'd choose, as I 'm alive,
Like a seat on the box, and a dashing drive!'
'Nay, PHAËTHON, don't, —
I beg you won't, —
Just stop a moment and think upon 't!'
'You 're quite too young,' continued the sage,
'To tend a coach at your tender age!
Besides, you see,
'T will really be
Your first appearance on any stage!
Desist, my child,
The cattle are wild,
And when their mettle is thoroughly "riled,"
Depend upon 't the coach 'll be "spiled," —
They 're not the fellows to draw it mild!
Desist, I say,
You 'll rue the day, —
To mind and don't be foolish, PHA!'
But the youth was proud,
And swore aloud,

'T was just the thing to astonish the crowd, —
He 'd have the horses and would n't be cowed!
In vain the boy was cautioned at large,
He called for the chargers, unheeding the charge,
And vowed that any young fellow of force
Could manage a dozen coursers, of course!
Now PHŒBUS felt exceedingly sorry
He had given his word in such a hurry,
But having sworn by the Styx, no doubt
He was in for it now, and could n't back out
So calling PHAËTHON up in a trice,
He gave the youth a bit of advice: —
'"*Parce stimulis, utere loris!*"
(A "stage direction," of which the core is,
Don't use the whip,— they 're ticklish things, —
But, whatever you do, hold on to the strings!)
Remember the rule of the Jehu-tribe is,
"*Medio tutissimus ibis*,"
(As the Judge remarked to a rowdy Scotchman,
Who was going to quod between two watchmen!)
So mind your eye, and spare your goad,
Be shy of the stones, and keep in the road!'

Now PHAËTHON, perched in the coachman's place,
Drove off the steeds at a furious pace,
Fast as coursers running a race,
Or bounding along in a steeple-chase!
Of whip and shout there was no lack,
'Crack — whack —
Whack — crack,'
Resounded along the horses' back! —

Frightened beneath the stinging lash,
Cutting their flanks in many a gash,
On — on they sped as swift as a flash,
Through thick and thin away they dash,
(Such rapid driving is always rash!)
When all at once, with a dreadful crash,
The whole 'establishment' went to smash!
    And PHAËTHON, he,
    As all agree,
Off the coach was suddenly hurled,
Into a puddle, and out of the world!

MORAL.

Don't rashly take to dangerous courses, —
Nor set it down in your table of forces,
That any one man equals any four horses
    Don't swear by the Styx! —
    It's one of OLD NICK'S
    Diabolical tricks
To get people into a regular 'fix,'
And hold 'em there as fast as bricks!

PYRAMUS AND THISBE.

This tragical tale, which, they say, is a true one,
Is old, but the manner is wholly a new one.
One *Ovid*, a writer of some reputation,
Has told it before in a tedious narration;
In a style, to be sure, of remarkable fulness,
But which nobody reads on account of its dulness.

Young Peter Pyramus — *I* call him *Peter*,
Not for the sake of the rhyme or metre,
But merely to make the name completer —
For Peter lived in the olden times,
And in one of the worst of Pagan climes
That flourish now in classical fame,
          Long before
          Either noble or boor
Had such a thing as a *Christian* name —
Young Peter then was a nice young beau
As any young lady would wish to know;
          In years, I ween,
          He was rather green,
That is to say, he was just eighteen, —
A trifle too short, and a shaving too lean,

But 'a nice young man' as ever was seen,
And fit to dance with a May-day queen!

Now PETER loved a beautiful girl
As ever insnared the heart of an earl
In the magical trap of an auburn curl,—
A little MISS THISBE who lived next door,
(They slept in fact on the very same floor,
With a wall between them, and nothing more,—
Those double dwellings were common of yore,)
And they loved each other, the legends say,
In that very beautiful, bountiful way,
That every young maid,
And every young blade,
Are wont to do before they grow staid,
And learn to love by the laws of trade.
But alack-a-day for the girl and boy,
A little impediment checked their joy,
And gave them, a while, the deepest annoy.
For some good reason, which history cloaks,
The match did n't happen to please the old folks!

So THISBE's father and PETER's mother
Began the young couple to worry and bother,
And tried their innocent passions to smother
By keeping the lovers from seeing each other!
But who ever heard
Of a marriage deterred,
Or even deferred,
By any contrivance so very absurd
As scolding the boy, and caging his bird?—

Now PETER, who was n't discouraged at all
By obstacles such as the timid appall,
Contrived to discover a hole in the wall,
Which was n't so thick
But removing a brick
Made a passage — though rather provokingly small
Through this little chink the lover could greet her,
And secrecy made their courting the sweeter,
While PETER kissed THISBE, and THISBE kissed PETER, —
For kisses, like folks with diminutive souls,
Will manage to creep through the smallest of holes

'T was here that the lovers, intent upon love,
Laid a nice little plot
To meet at a spot
Near a mulberry-tree in a neighboring grove;
For the plan was all laid,
By the youth and the maid,
(Whose hearts, it would seem, were uncommonly bold ones,)
To run off and get married in spite of the old ones.

In the shadows of evening, as still as a mouse,
The beautiful maiden slipt out of the house,
The mulberry-tree impatient to find,
While PETER, the vigilant matrons to blind,
Strolled leisurely out some minutes behind.

While waiting alone by the trysting tree,
  A terrible lion
  As e'er you set eye on,
Came roaring along quite horrid to see,
And caused the young maiden in terror to flee,
(A lion 's a creature whose regular trade is
Blood — and ' a terrible thing among ladies,')
And losing her veil as she ran from the wood,
The monster bedabbled it over with blood.

Now PETER arriving, and seeing the veil
  All covered o'er,
  And reeking with gore,
Turned all of a sudden exceedingly pale,
And sat himself down to weep and to wail, —
For, soon as he saw the garment, poor PETER
Made up his mind in very short metre,
That THISBE was dead, and the lion had eat her !
  So breathing a prayer,
  He determined to share
The fate of his darling, ' the loved and the lost,'
And fell on his dagger, and gave up the ghost !

Now THISBE returning, and viewing her beau,
Lying dead by the veil (which she happened to know),
She guessed, in a moment, the cause of his erring,
  And seizing the knife
  Which had taken his life,
In less than a jiffy was dead as a herring !

MORAL.

Young gentlemen! — pray recollect, if you please,
Not to make assignations near mulberry-trees;
Should your mistress be missing, it shows a weak head
To be stabbing yourself till you know she is dead.

Young ladies! — you should n't go strolling about
When your anxious mammas don't know you are out,
And remember that accidents often befall
From kissing young fellows through holes in the wall!

POLYPHEMUS AND ULYSSES.

A VERY remarkable history this is
Of one POLYPHEMUS and MR. ULYSSES;
The latter a hero accomplished and bold,
The former a knave and a fright to behold, —
A horrid big giant who lived in a den,
And dined every day on a couple of men,
Ate a woman for breakfast, and (dreadful to see!)
Had a nice little baby served up with his tea!
Indeed, if there 's truth in the sprightly narration
Of HOMER, a poet of some reputation,
Or VIRGIL, a writer but little inferior,
And in some things, perhaps, the other's superior,—
POLYPHEMUS was truly a terrible creature,
In manners and morals, in form and in feature;
For law and religion he cared not a copper,
And, in short, led a life that was very improper: —
What made him a very remarkable guy,
Like the late MR. THOMPSON, he 'd only one eye;
But that was a whopper, — a terrible one, —
'As large (VIRGIL says) as the disk of the sun!' —
A brilliant, but rather extravagant figure,
Which means, I suppose, that his eye was much
bigger

Than yours, — or even the orb of your sly
Old bachelor-friend who 's 'a wife in his eye.'

Ulysses, the hero I mentioned before,
Was shipwrecked, one day, on the pestilent shore
Where the Cyclops resided, along with their chief,
Polyphemus, the terrible man-eating thief,
Whose manners they copied, and laws they obeyed,
While driving their horrible cannibal trade

With many expressions of civil regret
That Ulysses had got so unpleasantly wet,
With many expressions of pleasure profound
That all had escaped being thoroughly drowned,
The rascal declared he was 'fond of the brave,'
And invited the strangers all home to his cave.

Here the cannibal king, with as little remorse
As an omnibus feels for the death of a horse,
Seized, crushed, and devoured a brace of the Greeks,
As a Welshman would swallow a couple of leeks,
Or a Frenchman, supplied with his usual prog,
Would punish the hams of a favorite frog.
Dashed and smashed against the stones,
He broke their bodies and cracked their bones,
Minding no more their moans and groans,
Than the grinder heeds his organ's tones!
With purple gore the pavement swims,
While the giant crushes their crackling limbs,

And poor ULYSSES trembles with fright
At the horrid sound, and the horrid sight, —
Trembles lest the monster grim
Should make his 'nuts and raisins' of him!
And, really, since
The man was a Prince,
It 's not very odd that his Highness should wince,
(Especially after such very strong hints,)
At the cannibal's manner, as rather more free
Than his Highness at court was accustomed to see!

But the crafty Greek, to the tyrant's hurt,
(Though he did n't deserve so fine a dessert,)
Took a dozen of wine from his leather trunk,
And plied the giant until he was drunk! —
Drunker than any one you or *I* know,
Who buys his 'Rhenish' with ready rhino, —
Exceedingly drunk, — '*sepultus vino!*'

Gazing a moment upon the sleeper,
ULYSSES cried, 'Let 's spoil his peeper! —
'T will put him, my boys, in a pretty trim,
If we can manage to douse his glim!'
So, taking a spar that was lying in sight,
They poked it into his 'forward light,'
And gouged away with furious spite,
Ramming and jamming with all their might!

In vain the giant began to roar,
And even swore
That he never before

Had met, in his life, such a terrible bore:
They only plied the auger the more
And mocked his grief with the bantering cry,
'Don't talk of pain, — *it 's all in your eye!*'
Until, alas for the wretched CYCLOPS!
He gives a groan, and out his eye pops!
Leaving the knave, one need n't be told,
As blind as a puppy of three days old.

The rest of the tale I can't tell now, —
Except that ULYSSES got out of the row,
With the rest of his crew — it 's no matter how;
While old POLYPHEMUS, until he was dead, —
Which was n't till many years after 't is said, —
Had a grief in his heart and a hole in his head!

MORAL.

Don't use strong drink, — pray let me advise, —
It 's bad for the stomach, and ruins the eyes;
Don't impose upon sailors with land-lubber tricks,
Or you 'll catch it some day like a thousand of bricks!

ORPHEUS AND EURYDICE.

SIR ORPHEUS, whom the poets have sung
In every metre and every tongue,
Was, you may remember, a famous musician, —
At least for a youth in his pagan condition, —
For historians tell he played on his shell
From morning till night, so remarkably well
That his music created a regular spell
On trees and stones in forest and dell!
What sort of an instrument his could be
Is really more than is known to me, —
For none of the books have told, d' ye see!
It 's very certain those heathen 'swells'
Knew nothing at all of oyster-shells,
And it's clear Sir Orpheus never could own a
Shell like those they make in Cremona;
But whatever it was, to 'move the stones'
It must have shelled out some powerful tones,
And entitled the player to rank in my rhyme
As the very *Vieuxtemps* of the very old time!

But alas for the joys of this mutable life!
Sir Orpheus lost his beautiful wife —

Eurydice — who vanished one day
From Earth, in a very unpleasant way!
It chanced, as near as I can determine,
Through one of those vertebrated vermin
That lie in the grass so prettily curled,
Waiting to 'snake' you out of the world!
And the poets tell she went to — well —
A place where Greeks and Romans dwell
After they burst their mortal shell;
A region that in the deepest shade is,
And known by the classical name of *Hades*, —
A different place from the terrible furnace
Of *Tartarus*, down below *Avernus*.

Now, having a heart uncommonly stout,
Sir Orpheus did n't go whining about,
Nor marry another, as *you* would, no doubt,
But made up his mind to fiddle her out!
But near the gate he had to wait,
For there in state old Cerberus sate, —
A three-headed dog, as cruel as Fate,
Guarding the entrance early and late;
A beast so sagacious, and very voracious,
So uncommonly sharp and extremely rapacious,
That it really may be doubted whether
He 'd have his match, should a common tether
Unite three aldermen's heads together!

But Orpheus, not in the least afraid,
Tuned up his shell, and quickly essayed
What could be done with a serenade.

In short, so charming an air he played,
He quite succeeded in overreaching
The cunning cur, by musical teaching,
And put him to sleep as fast as preaching!

And now our musical champion, Orpheus,
Having given the janitor over to Morpheus,
Went groping around among the ladies
Who throng the dismal halls of Hades,
Calling aloud
To the shady crowd,
In a voice as shrill as a martial fife,
'*O, tell me where in hell is my wife!*'
(A natural question, 't is very plain,
Although it may sound a little profane.)
'Eurydice! *Eu-ryd-i-ce!*'
He cried as loud as loud could be —
(A singular sound, and funny withal,
In a place where nobody *rides* at all!)
'Eurydice! — Eurydice!
O, come, my dear, along with me!'
And then he played so remarkably fine,
That it really might be called divine, —
For who can show,
On earth or below,
Such wonderful feats in the musical line?

E'en *Tantalus* ceased from trying to sip
The cup that flies from his arid lip;
Ixion, too, the magic could feel,
And, for a moment, blocked his wheel;

Poor *Sisyphus*, doomed to tumble and toss
The notable 'stone that gathers no moss,'
Let go his burden, and turned to hear
The charming sounds that ravished his ear;
And even the *Furies* — those terrible shrews
Whom no one before could ever amuse —
Those strong-bodied ladies with strong-minded views
Whom even the devil would doubtless refuse,
Were his majesty only permitted to choose —
Each felt for a moment her nature desert her,
And wept like a girl o'er the 'Sorrows of Werter

And still Sir Orpheus chanted his song,
Sweet and clear and strong and long,
'Eurydice! — Eurydice!'
He cried as loud as loud could be;
And Echo, taking up the word,
Kept it up till the lady heard,
And came with joy to meet her lord.
And he led her along the infernal route,
Until he had got her almost out,
When, suddenly turning his head about,
(To take a peep at his wife, no doubt,)
He gave a groan,
For the lady was gone,
And had left him standing there all alone!
For by an oath the gods had bound
Sir Orpheus not to look around
Till he was clear of the sacred ground,
If he 'd have Eurydice safe and sound,
For the moment he did an act so rash
His wife would vanish as quick as a flash!

MORAL.

Young women! beware, for goodness' sake,
Of every sort of 'sarpent snake;'
Remember the rogue is apt to deceive,
And played the deuse with grandmother Eve!
Young men! it 's a critical thing to go
Exactly right with a lady in tow;
But when you are in the proper track,
Just go ahead, and never look back!

THE MONEY-KING,

AND

OTHER POEMS.

1859.

To Mrs. George P. Marsh:

A Lady endowed with the best Gifts of Nature and Culture, and adorned with all Womanly Graces, — this volume is inscribed by her Friend,

The Author.

PREFACE.

About ten years ago, at the instance of my friend, James T. Fields, Esq., and with much misgiving, I ventured on the publication of a volume of poems. For the favor it has found with the public, — as evinced in a demand for sixteen editions of the book, — and with the critics, — as shown in many kind and scholarly reviews, — I take this occasion to express my grateful acknowledgments. Of the little which I have written since the first publication of that volume, the greater part will be found in this. In the arrangement of my materials, I have put "The Money-King" in front, simply on account of its length; as, in military usage, the tallest soldier is commonly placed at the head of the file. For the two episodes which interrupt the thread of this otherwise consecutive performance, I must plead the authority of greater names, ancient and modern. The poem entitled "The Way of the World," is little more than a paraphrase of a passage in a prose story lately published in Frazer's Magazine; and the plot of the Chinese Tale is mainly borrowed from an extremely clever English book, entitled "The Porcelain Tower." The rest of the pieces, for aught I can say, are as original as the verses of other men who have the misfortune to write at this rather late period in the history of letters; but if (as may possibly happen) any expressions which I have supposed to be my own should be found in the works of earlier writers, I can only answer, with the hearty indignation of old DONATUS: "*Pereant isti qui ante nostra dixerunt!*"

J. G. S.

THE MONEY-KING.

A POEM DELIVERED BEFORE THE PHI BETA KAPPA SOCIETY OF YALE COLLEGE, 1854.

As landsmen, sitting in luxurious ease,
Talk of the dangers of the stormy seas;
As fireside travellers, with portentous mien,
Tell tales of countries they have never seen;
As parlor-soldiers, graced with fancy-scars,
Rehearse their bravery in imagined wars;
As arrant dunces have been known to sit
In grave discourse of wisdom and of wit;
As paupers, gathered in congenial flocks,
Babble of banks, insurances, and stocks;
As each is oft'nest eloquent of what
He hates or covets, but possesses not; —
As cowards talk of pluck; misers, of waste;
Scoundrels, of honor; country clowns, of taste; —
I sing of MONEY! — no ignoble theme,
But loftier far than poetasters dream,
Whose fancies, soaring to their native moon,
Rise like a bubble or a gay balloon,
Whose orb aspiring takes a heavenward flight,
Just in proportion as it 's thin and light!

Kings must have Poets. From the earliest times,
Monarchs have loved celebrity in rhymes;
From good King *Robert*, who, in *Petrarch's* days,
Taught to mankind the proper use of bays,
And, singling out the prince of Sonneteers,
Twined wreaths of laurel 'round his blushing ears;
Down to the Queen, who, to her chosen bard,
In annual token of her kind regard,
Sends not alone the old poetic greens,
But, like a woman and the best of queens,
Adds to the leaves, to keep them fresh and fine,
The wholesome moisture of a pipe of wine! —
So may her minstrel, crowned with royal bays,
Alternate praise her pipe and pipe her praise!
E'en let him chant his smooth, euphonious lays:
A loftier theme my humbler Muse essays;
A mightier monarch be it hers to sing,
And claim her laurel from the Money-King!

Great was King Alfred; and if history state
His actions truly, good as well as great.
Great was the Norman; he whose martial hordes
Taught law and order to the Saxon lords,
With gentler thoughts their rugged minds imbued,
And raised the nation whom he first subdued.
Great was King Bess! — I see the critic smile,
As though the Muse mistook her proper style;
But to her purpose she will stoutly cling,
The royal maid was 'every inch a King'!
Great was Napoleon, — and I would that fate
Might prove his namesake-nephew half as great;

Meanwhile this hint I venture to advance: —
What France admires is good enough for France!
Great princes were they all; but greater far
Than English King, or mighty Russian Czar,
Or Pope of Rome, or haughty Queen of Spain,
Baron of Germany, or Royal Dane,
Or Gallic Emperor, or Persian Khan,
Or any other merely mortal man,
Is the great monarch that my Muse would sing,
That mighty potentate, the Money-King!
His kingdom vast extends o'er every land,
And nations bow before his high command;
The weakest tremble, and his power obey,
The strongest honor, and confess his sway.
He rules the Rulers! — e'en the tyrant Czar
Asks his permission ere he goes to war;
The Turk, submissive to his royal might,
By his consent has gracious leave to fight;
Whilst e'en Britannia makes her humblest bow
Before her Barings, not her Barons now,
Or on the Rothschild suppliantly calls,
(Her affluent 'uncle' with the golden balls,)
Begs of the Jew that he will kindly spare
Enough to put her trident in repair,
And pawns her diamonds, while she humbly craves
Leave of the Money-King once more to 'rule the waves'!

He wears no crown upon his royal head,
But many millions in his purse, instead;
He keeps no halls of state; but holds his court
In dingy rooms where greed and thrift resort;

In iron chests his wondrous wealth he hoards;
Banks are his parlors; brokers are his lords,
Bonds, bills, and mortgages, his favorite books,
Gold is his food, and coiners are his cooks;
Ledgers his records; stock-reports his news;
Merchants his yeomen, and his bondsmen Jews;
Kings are his subjects, gamblers are his knaves,
Spendthrifts his fools, and misers are his slaves!
The good, the bad, his golden favor prize,
The high, the low, the simple, and the wise,
The young, the old, the stately, and the gay, —
All bow obedient to his royal sway!

See where, afar, the bright Pacific shore
Gleams in the sun with sands of shining ore,
His last, great empire rises to the view,
And shames the wealth of India and Peru!
Here, throned within his gorgeous "golden gate,"
He wields his sceptre o'er the rising State;
Surveys his conquest with a joyful eye,
Nor for a greater heaves a single sigh!
Here, quite beyond the classic poet's dream,
Pactolus runs in every winding stream;
The mountain cliffs the glittering ore enfold,
And every reed that rustles whispers, 'gold!'

If to his sceptre some dishonor clings,
Why should we marvel? — 't is the fate of Kings!
Their power too oft perverted by abuse,
Their manners cruel, or their morals loose,
The best at times have wandered far astray
From simple Virtue's unseductive way;

And few, of all, at once could make pretence
To royal robes and rustic innocence!

He builds the house where Christian people pray,
And rears a bagnio just across the way;
Pays to the priest his stinted annual fee;
Rewards the lawyer for his venal plea;
Sends an apostle to the heathen's aid;
And cheats the Choctaws, for the good of trade;
Lifts by her heels an Ellsler to renown,
Or, bribing 'Jenny,' brings an angel down!
He builds the Theatres, and gambling Halls,
Lloyds and Almacks, St. Peter's and St. Paul's;
Sin's gay retreats, and Fashion's gilded rooms,
Hotels and Factories, Palaces and Tombs;
Bids Commerce spread her wings to every gale;
Bends to the breeze the pirate's bloody sail;
Helps Science seek new worlds among the stars;
Profanes our own with mercenary wars;
The friend of wrong, the equal friend of right,
Oft may we bless and oft deplore his might,
As buoyant hope or darkening fears prevail,
And good or evil turns the moral scale.

All fitting honor I would fain accord,
Whene'er he builds a temple to the Lord;
But much I grieve he often spends his pelf,
As it were raised in honor of himself;
Or, what were worse, and more profanely odd,
A place to worship some Egyptian god!
I wish his favorite architects were graced
With sounder judgment, and a Christian taste.

Immortal Wren! what fierce, convulsive shocks
Would jar thy bones within their leaden box,
Couldst thou but look across the briny spray,
And see some churches of the present day! —
The lofty dome of consecrated bricks,
Where all the 'orders' in disorder mix,
To form a temple whose incongruous frame
Confounds design and puts the Arts to shame!
Where 'styles' discordant on the vision jar,
Where Greek and Roman are again at war,
And, as of old, the unrelenting Goth
Comes down at last and overwhelms them both!

Once on a time I heard a parson say,
(Talking of churches in a sprightly way,)
That there was more Religion in the walls
Of towering 'Trinity,' or grand 'St. Paul's,'
Than one could find, upon the strictest search,
In half the saints within the Christian Church!
A layman sitting at the parson's side
To this new dogma thus at once replied: —
'If, as you say, Religion has her home
In the mere walls that form the sacred dome,
It seems to me the very plainest case,
To climb the steeple were a growth in grace;
And he to whom the pious strength were given
To reach the highest were the nearest Heaven!
I thought the answer just; and yet 't is clear
A solemn aspect, grand and yet severe,
Becomes the house of God. 'T is hard to say
Who from the proper mark are most astray, —

They who erect, for holy Christian rites,
A gay Pagoda with its tinsel lights,
Or they who offer to the God of Love
A gorgeous Temple of the pagan Jove!

Immortal Homer and Tassoni sing
What vast results from trivial causes spring;
How naughty Helen by her stolen joy
Brought woe and ruin to unhappy Troy;
How, for a bucket, rash Bologna sold
More blood and tears than twenty such could hold
Thy power, O Money, shows results as strange
As aught revealed in History's widest range;
Thy smallest coin of shining silver shows
More potent magic than a conjurer knows!
In olden times, — if classic poets say
The simple truth, as poets do to-day, —
When Charon's boat conveyed a spirit o'er
The Lethean water to the Hadean shore,
The fare was just a penny, — not too great,
The moderate, regular, Stygian statute rate.
Now, for a shilling, he will cross the stream,
(His paddles whirling to the force of steam!)
And bring, obedient to some wizard power,
Back to the Earth more spirits in an hour,
Than Brooklyn's famous ferry could convey.
Or thine, Hoboken, in the longest day!
Time was when men bereaved of vital breath
Were calm and silent in the realms of Death;
When mortals dead and decently inurned
Were heard no more; no traveller returned.

Who once had crossed the dark Plutonian strand,
To whisper secrets of the spirit-land —
Save when perchance some sad, unquiet soul
Among the tombs might wander on parole, —
A well-bred ghost, at night's bewitching noon,
Returned to catch some glimpses of the moon,
Wrapt in a mantle of unearthly white,
(The only *'rapping* of an ancient sprite!)
Stalked round in silence till the break of day,
Then from the Earth passed unperceived away!
  Now all is changed: the musty maxim fails,
And dead men *do* repeat the queerest tales!
Alas, that here, as in the books, we see
The travellers clash, the doctors disagree!
Alas, that all, the further they explore,
For all their search are but confused the more!
  Ye great departed! — men of mighty mark —
Bacon and Newton, Adams, Adam Clarke,
Edwards and Whitefield, Franklin, Robert Hall,
Calhoun, Clay, Channing, Daniel Webster — all
Ye great quit-tenants of this earthly ball, —
If in your new abodes ye cannot rest,
But must return, O, grant us this request:
Come with a noble and celestial air,
To prove your title to the names ye bear;
Give some clear token of your heavenly birth;
Write as good English as ye wrote on Earth!
Show not to all, in ranting prose and verse,
The spirit's progress is from bad to worse;
And, what were once superfluous to advise,
Don't tell, I beg you, such egregious lies! —

Or if perchance your agents are to blame,
Don't let them trifle with your honest fame;
Let chairs and tables rest, and 'rap' instead,
Ay, 'knock' your slippery 'Mediums' on the head!

What direful woes the hapless man attend,
Who in the means see life's supremest end;
The wretched miser, — money's sordid slave, —
His only joy to gather and to save.
For this he wakes at morning's early light,
Toils through the day, and ponders in the night;
For this, — to swell his heap of tarnished gold, —
Sweats in the sun, and shivers in the cold,
And suffers more from hunger every day
Than the starved beggar whom he spurns away.
Death comes erewhile to end his worldly strife;
With all his saving he must lose his life!
Perchance the Doctor might protract his breath,
And stay the dreadful messenger of death;
But none is there to comfort or advise;
'T would cost a dollar! — so the miser dies.

Sad is the sight when Money's power controls
In wedlock's chains the fate of human souls.
From mine to mint, curst is the coin that parts
In helpless grief two loving human hearts;
Or joins in discord, jealousy, and hate,
A sordid suitor to a loathing mate!
I waive the case, the barren case, of those
Who have no hearts to cherish or to lose;
Whose wedded state is but a bargain made
In due accordance with the laws of trade:

When the prim parson joins their willing hands,
To marry City lots to Western lands,
Or in connubial ecstasy to mix
Cash and 'collateral,' ten-per-cents with six,
And in soft dalliance securely locks
Impassioned dollars with enamored stocks,
Laugh if you will, — and who can well refrain? —
But waste no tears, nor pangs of pitying pain;
Hearts such as these may play the queerest pranks,
But never break — except with breaking banks!

Yet, let me hint, a thousand maxims prove
Plutus may be the truest friend to *Love.*
'Love in a cottage' cosily may dwell,
But much prefers to have it furnished well!
A parlor ample, and a kitchen snug,
A handsome carpet, an embroidered rug,
A well-stored pantry, and a tidy maid,
A blazing hearth, a cooling window-shade
Though merely mortal, money-purchased things,
Have wondrous power to clip Love's errant wings!
'Love in a cottage,' is n't just the same,
When wind and water strive to quench his flame;
Too oft it breeds the sharpest discontent,
That puzzling question, 'how to pay the rent;'
A smoky chimney may alone suffice
To dim the radiance of the fondest eyes;
A northern blast, beyond the slightest doubt,
May fairly blow the torch of *Hymen* out;
And I have heard a worthy matron hold,
(As one who knew the truth of what she told,)

Love once was drowned, though reckoned water-
proof,
By the mere dripping of a leaky roof!

Full many a wise philosopher has tried
Mankind in fitting orders to divide;
And by their forms, their fashions, and their face,
To group, assort, and classify the race.
One would distinguish people by their books;
Another, quaintly, solely by their cooks;
And one, who graced the philosophic bench,
Found these three classes, — 'women, men, and
French!'
The best remains, of all that I have known,
A broad distinction, brilliant, and my own, —
Of all mankind, I classify the lot: —
Those who *have Money*, and those who have *not*!

Think'st thou the line a poet's fiction? — then
Go look abroad upon the ways of men!
Go ask the banker, with his golden seals;
Go ask the borrower, cringing at his heels;
Go ask the maid who, emulous of woe,
Discards the worthier for the wealthier beau;
Go ask the Parson, when a higher prize
Points with the salary where his *duty* lies;
Go ask the Lawyer, who, in legal smoke,
Stands, like a stoker, redolent of "Coke,"
And swings his arms to emphasize a plea
Made doubly ardent by a golden fee;
Go ask the Doctor, who has kindly sped
Old Crœsus, dying on a damask bed,

While his poor neighbor — wonderful to tell —
Was left to Nature, suffered, and got well!
Go ask the belle, in high patrician pride,
Who spurns the maiden nurtured at her side,
Her youth's loved playmate at the village-school,
Ere changing fortune taught the rigid rule
Which marks the loftier from the lowlier lot, —
Those who have money from those who have not!

Of all the ills that owe their baneful rise
To wealth o'ergrown, the most despotic vice
Is Circean Luxury; prolific dame
Of mental impotence, and moral shame,
And all the cankering evils that debase
The human form, and dwarf the human race.
See yon strange figure, and a moment scan
That slenderest sample of the genus man!
Mark, as he ambles, those precarious pegs
Which by their motion must be deemed his legs!
He has a head, — one may be sure of that
By just observing that he wears a hat;
That he has arms is logically plain
From his wide coat-sleeves and his pendant cane
A tongue as well, — the inference is fair,
Since, on occasion, he can lisp and swear.
You ask his use? — that 's not so very clear,
Unless to spend five thousand pounds a year
In modish vices which his soul adores,
Drink, dress, and gaming, horses, hounds, and scores
Of other follies which I can't rehearse,
Dear to himself and dearer to his purse.

No product he of Fortune's fickle dice
The due result of Luxury and Vice,
Three generations have sufficed to bring
That narrow-chested, pale, enervate thing
Down from a *man*, — for, marvel as you will,
His huge great-grandsire fought on Bunker-Hill!
Bore, without gloves, a musket through the war;
Came back adorned with many a noble scar;
Labored and prospered at a thriving rate,
And, dying, left his heir a snug estate, —
Which grew apace upon *his* busy hands,
Stocks, ships, and factories, tenements and lands,
All here at last — the money and the race —
The latter ending in that foolish face;
The former wandering, far beyond his aim,
Back to the rough plebeians whence it came!

Enough of censure; let my humble lays
Employ one moment in congenial praise.
Let other pens with pious ardor paint
The selfish virtues of the cloistered saint;
In lettered marble let the stranger read
Of him who, dying, did a worthy deed,
And left to charity the cherished store
Which, to his sorrow, he could hoard no more.
I venerate the nobler man who gives
His generous dollars while the donor lives;
Gives with a heart as liberal as the palms
That to the needy spread his honored alms;
Gives with a head whose yet unclouded light
To worthiest objects points the giver's sight;

Gives with a hand still potent to enforce
His well-aimed bounty, and direct its course; —
Such is the giver who must stand confest
In giving glorious, and supremely blest!
One such as this the captious world could find
In noble Perkins, angel of the blind;
One such as this in princely Lawrence shone,
Ere heavenly kindred claimed him for their own!

To me the boon may gracious Heaven assign, —
No cringing suppliant at Mammon's shrine,
Nor slave of Poverty, — with joy to share
The happy mean expressed in Agur's prayer: —
A house (my own) to keep me safe and warm,
A shade in sunshine, and a shield in storm;
A generous board, and fitting raiment, clear
Of debts and duns throughout the circling year;
Silver and gold, in moderate store, that I
May purchase joys that only these can buy;
Some gems of art, a cultured mind to please,
Books, pictures, statues, literary ease.
That 'Time is Money' prudent Franklin shows
In rhyming couplets, and sententious prose.
O, had he taught the world, in prose and rhyme,
The higher truth that Money may be Time!
And showed the people, in his pleasant ways,
The art of coining dollars into days!
Days for improvement, days for social life,
Days for your God, your children, and your wife;
Some days for pleasure, and an hour to spend
In genial converse with an honest friend.

Such days be mine! — and grant me, Heaven, but
this,
With blooming health, man's highest earthly bliss, —
And I will read, without a sigh or frown,
The startling news that stocks are going down;
Hear without envy that a stranger hoards
Or spends more treasure than a mint affords;
See my next neighbor pluck a golden plum,
Calm and content within my cottage-home;
Take for myself what honest thrift may bring,
And for his kindness, bless the Money-King!

I'M GROWING OLD.

My days pass pleasantly away;
  My nights are blest with sweetest sleep;
I feel no symptoms of decay;
  I have no cause to mourn nor weep;
My foes are impotent and shy;
  My friends are neither false nor cold,
And yet, of late, I often sigh, —
            I 'm growing old!

My growing talk of olden times,
  My growing thirst for early news
My growing apathy to rhymes,
  My growing love of easy shoes,
My growing hate of crowds and noise,
  My growing fear of taking cold,
All whisper, in the plainest voice,
            I 'm growing old!

I 'm growing fonder of my staff;
  I 'm growing dimmer in the eyes;
I 'm growing fainter in my laugh;
  I 'm grewing deeper in my sighs;

I 'm growing careless of my dress ;
  I 'm growing frugal of my gold ;
I 'm growing wise ; I 'm growing — yes —
          I 'm growing old !

I see it in my changing taste ;
  I see it in my changing hair ;
I see it in my growing waist ;
  I see it in my growing heir ;
A thousand signs proclaim the truth,
  As plain as truth was ever told,
That, even in my vaunted youth,
          I 'm growing old !

Ah me ! — my very laurels breathe
  The tale in my reluctant ears,
And every boon the Hours bequeath
  But makes me debtor to the Years !
E'en Flattery's honeyed words declare
  The secret she would fain withhold,
And tells me in ' How young you are ! '
          I 'm growing old !

Thanks for the years ! — whose rapid flight
  My sombre Muse too sadly sings ;
Thanks for the gleams of golden light
  That tint the darkness of their wings ;
The light that beams from out the sky,
  Those Heavenly mansions to unfold
Where all are blest, and none may sigh,
          ' I 'm growing old ! '

SPES EST VATES.

THERE is a saying of the ancient sages:
  No noble human thought,
However buried in the dust of ages,
  Can ever come to naught.

With kindred faith, that knows no base dejection,
  Beyond the sages' scope
I see, afar, the final resurrection
  Of every glorious hope.

I see, as parcel of a new creation,
  The beatific hour
When every bud of lofty aspiration
  Shall blossom into flower.

We are not mocked; it was not in derision
  God made our spirits free;
The poet's dreams are but the dim prevision
  Of blessings that shall be,—

When they who lovingly have hoped and trusted,
  Despite some transient fears,
Shall see Life's jarring elements adjusted,
  And rounded into spheres!

THE WAY OF THE WORLD.

I.

A YOUTH would marry a maiden,
  For fair and fond was she;
But she was rich, and he was poor,
  And so it might not be.
    A lady never could wear—
      Her mother held it firm—
    A gown that came of an India plant,
      Instead of an India worm!—
And so the cruel word was spoken;
And so it was two hearts were broken.

II.

A youth would marry a maiden,
  For fair and fond was she;
But he was high and she was low,
  And so it might not be.
    A man who had worn a spur,
      In ancient battle won,
    Had sent it down with great renown,
      To goad his future son!—
And so the cruel word was spoken;
And so it was two hearts were broken.

III.

A youth would marry a maiden,
For fair and fond was she;
But their sires disputed about the Mass,
And so it might not be.
A couple of wicked Kings,
Three hundred years agone,
Had played at a royal game of chess,
And the church had been a pawn!—
And so the cruel word was spoken;
And so it was two hearts were broken.

THE HEAD AND THE HEART.

THE head is stately, calm, and wise,
  And bears a princely part;
And down below in secret lies
  The warm, impulsive heart.

The lordly head that sits above,
  The heart that beats below,
Their several office plainly prove,
  Their true relation show.

The head erect, serene, and cool,
  Endowed with Reason's art,
Was set aloft to guide and rule
  The throbbing, wayward heart.

And from the head, as from the higher,
  Comes every glorious thought;
And in the heart's transforming fire
  All noble deeds are wrought.

Yet each is best when both unite
  To make the man complete;
What were the heat without the light?
  The light, without the heat?

MY CASTLE IN SPAIN.

THERE 's a castle in Spain, very charming to see,
Though built without money or toil;
Of this handsome estate I am owner in fee,
And paramount lord of the soil;
And oft as I may I 'm accustomed to go
And live, like a king, in my Spanish Chateau!

There 's a dame most bewitchingly rounded and ripe,
Whose wishes are never absurd;
Who does n't object to my smoking a pipe,
Nor insist on the ultimate word;
In short, she 's the pink of perfection, you know;
And she lives, like a queen, in my Spanish Chateau!

I 've a family too; the delightfulest girls,
And a bevy of beautiful boys;
All quite the reverse of those juvenile churls
Whose pleasure is mischief and noise;
No modern *Cornelia* might venture to show
Such jewels as those in my Spanish Chateau!

I have servants who seek their contentment in mine,
  And always mind what they are at;
Who never embezzle the sugar and wine,
  And slander the innocent cat;
Neither saucy, nor careless, nor stupidly slow,
Are the servants who wait in my Spanish Chateau!

I have pleasant companions; most affable folk;
  And each with the heart of a brother;
Keen wits, who enjoy an antagonist's joke;
  And beauties who 're fond of each other;
Such people, indeed, as you never may know,
Unless you should come to my Spanish Chateau!

I have friends, whose commission for wearing the name
  In kindness unfailing is shown;
Who pay to another the duty they claim,
  And deem his successes their own;
Who joy in his gladness, and weep at his woe;
You 'll find them (where else?) in my Spanish Chateau!

'*O si sic semper!*' I oftentimes say,
  (Though 't is idle, I know, to complain,)
To think that again I must force me away
  From my beautiful castle in Spain!
Ah! would that my stars had determined it so
I might live the year round in my Spanish Chateau!

A REFLECTIVE RETROSPECT.

'Tis twenty years, and something more,
  Since, all athirst for useful knowledge,
I took some draughts of classic lore,
  Drawn very mild, at ——rd College;
Yet I remember all that one
  Could wish to hold in recollection;
The boys, the joys, the noise, the fun;
  But not a single Conic Section.

I recollect those harsh affairs,
  The morning bells that gave us panics,
I recollect the formal prayers,
  That seemed like lessons in Mechanics;
I recollect the drowsy way
  In which the students listened to them,
As clearly, in my wig, to-day,
  As when, a boy, I slumbered through them.

I recollect the tutors all
  As freshly now, if I may say so,
As any chapter I recall
  In Homer or Ovidius Naso.

I recollect, extremely well,
  'Old Hugh,' the mildest of fanatics;
I well remember Matthew Bell,
  But very faintly, Mathematics.

I recollect the prizes paid
  For lessons fathomed to the bottom;
(Alas that pencil-marks should fade!)
  I recollect the chaps who got 'em, —
The light equestrians who soared
  O'er every passage reckoned stony;
And took the chalks, — but never scored
  A single honor to the pony!

Ah me! — what changes Time has wrought,
  And how predictions have miscarried!
A few have reached the goal they sought,
  And some are dead, and some are married!
And some in city journals war;
  And some as politicians bicker;
And some are pleading at the bar —
  For jury-verdicts, or for liquor!

And some on Trade and Commerce wait;
  And some in schools with dunces battle;
And some the Gospel propagate;
  And some the choicest breeds of cattle;
And some are living at their ease;
  And some were wrecked in 'the revulsion;'
Some serve the State for handsome fees,
  And one, I hear, upon compulsion!

LAMONT, who, in his college days,
  Thought e'en a cross a moral scandal,
Has left his Puritanic ways,
  And worships now with bell and candle;
And MANN, who mourned the negro's fate,
  And held the slave as most unlucky,
Now holds him, at the market rate,
  On a plantation in Kentucky!

TOM KNOX — who swore in such a tone
  It fairly might be doubted whether
It really was himself alone,
  Or *Knox* and Erebus together —
Has grown a very altered man,
  And, changing oaths for mild entreaty,
Now recommends the Christian plan
  To savages in Otaheite!

Alas for young ambition's vow!
  How envious Fate may overthrow it! —
Poor HARVEY is in Congress now,
  Who struggled long to be a poet;
SMITH carves (quite well) memorial stones,
  Who tried in vain to make the law go;
HALL deals in hides; and "Pious Jones"
  Is dealing faro in Chicago!

And, sadder still, the brilliant HAYS,
  Once honest, manly, and ambitious,
Has taken latterly to ways
  Extremely profligate and vicious;

By slow degrees — I can't tell how —
  He 's reached at last the very groundsel,
And in New York he figures now,
  A member of the Common Council!

'DO YOU THINK HE IS MARRIED?

MADAM, — you are very pressing,
  And I can't decline the task;
With the slightest gift of guessing,
  You would scarcely need to ask!

Don't you see a hint of marriage
  In his sober-sided face?
In his rather careless carriage,
  And extremely rapid pace?

If he 's not committed treason,
  Or some wicked action done,
Can you see the faintest reason
  Why a bachelor should run?

Why should *he* be in a flurry?
  But a loving wife to greet
Is a circumstance to hurry
  The most dignified of feet!

When afar the man has spied her,
  If the grateful, happy elf
Does not haste to be beside her,
  He must be beside himself!

It is but a trifle, maybe,—
  But observe his practised tone,
When he calms your stormy baby,
  Just as if it were his own!

Do you think a certain meekness
  You have mentioned in his looks,
Is a chronic optic weakness
  That has come of reading books?

Did you ever see his vision
  Peering underneath a hood,
Save enough for recognition,
  As a civil person should!

Could a Capuchin be colder
  When he glances, as he must,
At a finely-rounded shoulder,
  Or a proudly-swelling bust?

Madam!—think of every feature,
  Then deny it, if you can,
He's a fond, connubial creature,
  And a *very* married man!

EARLY RISING.

'God bless the man who first invented sleep!'
So Sancho Panza said, and so say I:
And bless him, also, that he did n't keep
His great discovery to himself; nor try
To make it — as the lucky fellow might —
A close monopoly by patent-right!

Yes — bless the man who first invented sleep,
(I really can't avoid the iteration;)
But blast the man, with curses loud and deep,
Whate'er the rascal's name, or age, or station,
Who first invented, and went round advising,
That artificial cut-off — Early Rising!

'Rise with the lark, and with the lark to bed,'
Observes some solemn, sentimental owl;
Maxims like these are very cheaply said;
But, ere you make yourself a fool or fowl,
Pray just inquire about his rise and fall,
And whether larks have any beds at all!

'The time for honest folks to be a-bed'
Is in the morning, if I reason right;
And he who cannot keep his precious head
Upon his pillow till it 's fairly light,

And so enjoy his forty morning winks,
Is up to knavery; or else — he drinks!

Thomson, who sung about the 'Seasons,' said
  It was a glorious thing to *rise* in season;
But then he said it — lying — in his bed,
  At ten o'clock A. M., — the very reason
He wrote so charmingly. The simple fact is,
His preaching was n't sanctioned by his practice.

'T is, doubtless, well to be sometimes awake, —
  Awake to duty, and awake to truth, —
But when, alas! a nice review we take
  Of our best deeds and days, we find, in sooth,
The hours that leave the slightest cause to weep
Are those we passed in childhood or asleep!

'T is beautiful to leave the world awhile
  For the soft visions of the gentle night;
And free, at last, from mortal care or guile,
  To live as only in the angels' sight,
In sleep's sweet realm so cosily shut in,
Where, at the worst, we only *dream* of sin!

So let us sleep, and give the Maker praise.
  I like the lad who, when his father thought
To clip his morning nap by hackneyed phrase
  Of vagrant worm by early songster caught,
Cried, 'Served him right! — it 's not at all surprising;
The worm was punished, sir, for early rising!'

IDEAL AND REAL.

IDEAL.

SOME years ago, when I was young,
And Mrs. Jones was Miss Delancy;
When wedlock's canopy was hung
With curtains from the loom of fancy;
I used to paint my future life
With most poetical precision, —
My special wonder of a wife;
My happy days; my nights Elysian.

I saw a lady, rather small,
(A JUNO was my strict abhorrence,)
With flaxen hair, contrived to fall
In careless ringlets, *à la* Lawrence;
A blonde complexion; eyes that drew
From autumn clouds their azure brightness;
The foot of Venus; arms whose hue
Was perfect in its milky whiteness!

I saw a party, quite select, —
There might have been a baker's dozen;
A parson, of the ruling sect;
A bridemaid, and a city cousin;

A formal speech to me and mine,
  (Its meaning I could scarce discover;)
A taste of cake; a sip of wine;
  Some kissing — and the scene was over!

I saw a baby — one — no more;
  A cherub pictured, rather faintly,
Beside a pallid dame who wore
  A countenance extremely saintly.
I saw, — but nothing could I hear,
  Except the softest prattle, maybe,
The merest breath upon the ear, —
  So quiet was that blessèd baby!

REAL.

I see a woman, rather tall,
  And yet, I own, a comely lady;
Complexion — such as I must call
  (To be exact) a little shady;
A hand not handsome, yet confessed
  A generous one for love or pity;
A nimble foot, and — neatly dressed
  In No. 5 — extremely pretty!

I see a group of boys and girls
  Assembled round the knee paternal;
With ruddy cheeks and tangled curls,
  And manners not at all supernal.

And one has reached a manly size;
  And one aspires to woman's stature;
And one is quite a recent prize,
  And all abound in human nature!

The boys are hard to keep in trim;
  The girls are often rather trying;
And baby — like the cherubim —
  Seems very fond of steady crying!
And yet the precious little one,
  His mother's dear, despotic master,
Is worth a thousand babies done
  In Parian or in alabaster!

And oft that stately dame and I,
  When laughing o'er our early dreaming,
And marking, as the years go by,
  How idle was our youthful scheming,
Confess the wiser Power that knew
  How *Duty* every joy enhances,
And gave us blessings rich and true,
  And better far than all our fancies!

HOW THE MONEY GOES.

How goes the Money? — Well,
I'm sure it is n't hard to tell;
It goes for rent, and water-rates,
For bread and butter, coal and grates,
Hats, caps, and carpets, hoops and hose, —
And that's the way the Money goes!

How goes the Money? — Nay,
Don't everybody know the way?
It goes for bonnets, coats, and capes,
Silks, satins, muslins, velvets, crapes,
Shawls, ribbons, furs, and furbelows, —
And that's the way the Money goes!

How goes the Money? — Sure,
I wish the ways were something fewer;
It goes for wages, taxes, debts;
It goes for presents, goes for bets,
For paint, *pommade*, and *eau de rose*, —
And that's the way the Money goes!

How goes the Money? — Now,
I've scarce begun to mention how;

It goes for laces, feathers, rings,
Toys, dolls — and other baby-things,
Whips, whistles, candies, bells, and bows, —
And that 's the way the Money goes!

How goes the Money? — Come,
I know it does n't go for rum;
It goes for schools and Sabbath chimes,
It goes for charity — sometimes;
For missions, and such things as those, —
And that 's the way the Money goes!

How goes the Money? — There!
I 'm out of patience, I declare;
It goes for plays, and diamond-pins,
For public alms, and private sins,
For hollow shams, and silly shows, —
And that 's the way the Money goes!

TALE OF A DOG.

IN TWO PARTS.

PART FIRST.

I.

'Curse on all curs!' I heard a cynic cry;
  A wider malediction than he thought, —
For what's a cynic? — Had he cast his eye
  Within his dictionary, he had caught
This much of learning, — the untutored elf, —
That he, unwittingly, had cursed himself!

II.

'Beware of dogs,' the great Apostle writes;
  A rather brief and sharp philippic sent
To the Philippians. The paragraph invites
  Some little question as to its intent,
Among the best expositors; but then
I find they all agree that "dogs" meant *men!*

III.

Beware of men! a moralist might say,
  And women too; 't were but a prudent hint,
Well worth observing in a general way,
  But having surely no conclusion in 't,
(As saucy satirists are wont to rail,)
All men are faithless, and all women frail.

IV.

And so of dogs 't were wrong to dogmatize
 Without discrimination or degree;
For one may see, with half a pair of eyes,
 That they have characters as well as we:
I hate the rascal who can walk the street
Caning all canines he may chance to meet.

V.

I had a dog that was not all a dog,
 For in his nature there was something human;
Wisely he looked as any pedagogue;
 Loved funerals and weddings, like a woman;
With this (still human) weakness, I confess,
Of always judging people by their dress.

VI.

He hated beggars, it was very clear,
 And oft was seen to drive them from the door;
But that was education; — for a year,
 Ere yet his puppyhood was fairly o'er,
He lived with a Philanthropist, and caught
His practices; the precepts he forgot!

VII.

Which was a pity; yet the dog, I grant,
 Led, on the whole, a very worthy life.
To teach you industry, 'Go to the ant,'
 (I mean the insect, not your uncle's wife;)
But — though the counsel sounds a little rude —
Go to the dogs, for love and gratitude.

PART SECOND.

VIII.

'Throw physic to the dogs,' the poet cries;
  A downright insult to the canine race;
There 's not a puppy but is far too wise
  To put a pill or powder in his face.
Perhaps the poet merely meant to say,
That physic, thrown to dogs, is thrown away, —

IX.

Which (as the parson said about the dice)
  Is the best throw that any man can choose;
Take, if you 're ailing, medical advice, —
  Minus the medicine — which, of course, refuse.
Drugging, no doubt, occasioned Homœopathy,
And all the dripping horrors of Hydropathy.

X.

At all events, 't is fitting to remark,
  Dogs spurn at drugs; their daily bark and whine
Are not at all the musty wine and bark
  The doctors give to patients in decline;
And yet a dog who felt a fracture's smart
Once thanked a kind chirurgeon for his art.

XI.

I 've heard a story, and believe it true,
  About a dog that chanced to break his leg;
His master set it and the member grew
  Once more a sound and serviceable peg;
And how d' ye think the happy dog exprest
The grateful feelings of his glowing breast?

XII.

'T was not in words; the customary pay
  Of human debtors for a friendly act;
For dogs their thoughts can neither sing nor say
  E'en in "dog-latin," which (a curious fact)
Is spoken only — as a classic grace —
By grave Professors of the human race!

XIII.

No, 't was in deed; the very briefest tail
  Declared his deep emotions at his cure;
Short, but significant; — one could not fail,
  From the mere wagging of his cynosure
('Surgens e *puppi*'), and his ears agog,
To see the fellow was a grateful dog!

XIV.

One day — still mindful of his late disaster —
  He wandered off the village to explore;
And brought another dog unto his master,
  Lame of a leg, as he had been before;
As who should say, 'You see! — the dog is lame
You doctored me, pray, doctor him the same!'

XV.

So runs the story, and you have it cheap, —
  Dog-cheap, as doubtless such a tale should be;
The moral, surely, is n't hard to reap: —
  Be prompt to listen unto mercy's plea;
The good you get, diffuse; it will not hurt you
E'en from a dog to learn a Christian virtue!

LITTLE JERRY, THE MILLER.

A BALLAD.

BENEATH the hill you may see the mill
  Of wasting wood and crumbling stone;
The wheel is dripping and clattering still,
  But JERRY, the miller, is dead and gone.

Year after year, early and late,
  Alike in summer and winter weather,
He pecked the stones and calked the gate,
  And mill and miller grew old together.

'Little Jerry!'—'t was all the same,—
  They loved him well who called him so;
And whether he 'd ever another name,
  Nobody ever seemed to know.

'T was 'Little Jerry, come grind my rye;'
  And 'Little Jerry, come grind my wheat;'
And 'Little Jerry' was still the cry,
  From matron bold and maiden sweet.

'T was 'Little Jerry' on every tongue,
  And so the simple truth was told;
For Jerry was little when he was young,
  And Jerry was little when he was old.

But what in size he chanced to lack,
  That Jerry made up in being strong;
I've seen a sack upon his back
  As thick as the miller, and quite as long.

Always busy, and always merry,
  Always doing his very best,
A notable wag was Little Jerry,
  Who uttered well his standing jest.

How Jerry lived is known to fame,
  But how he died there's none may know;
One autumn day the rumor came,
  'The brook and Jerry are very low.'

And then 't was whispered, mournfully,
  The leech had come, and he was dead;
And all the neighbors flocked to see;
  'Poor Little Jerry!' was all they said.

They laid him in his earthy bed,—
  His miller's coat his only shroud;
"Dust to dust," the parson said,
  And all the people wept aloud.

For he had shunned the deadly sin,
  And not a grain of over-toll
Had ever dropped into his bin,
  To weigh upon his parting soul.

Beneath the hill there stands the mill,
  Of wasting wood and crumbling stone;
The wheel is dripping and clattering still,
  But JERRY, the miller, is dead and gone.

HOW CYRUS LAID THE CABLE

A BALLAD.

COME, listen all unto my song;
  It is no silly fable;
'T is all about the mighty cord
  They call the Atlantic Cable.

Bold Cyrus Field he said, says he,
  I have a pretty notion
That I can run a telegraph
  Across the Atlantic Ocean.

Then all the people laughed, and said,
  They 'd like to see him do it;
He might get half-seas-over, but
  He never could go through it;

To carry out his foolish plan
  He never would be able;
He might as well go hang himself
  With his Atlantic Cable!

But Cyrus was a valiant man,
  A fellow of decision;
And heeded not their mocking words,
  Their laughter and derision.

Twice did his bravest efforts fail,
  And yet his mind was stable;
He wa'n't the man to break his heart
  Because he broke his cable.

'Once more, my gallant boys!' he cried;
  '*Three times!* — you know the fable, —
(I'll make it *thirty*,' muttered he,
  'But I will lay the cable!')

Once more they tried, — hurrah! hurrah!
  What means this great commotion?
The Lord be praised! the cable's laid
  Across the Atlantic Ocean!

Loud ring the bells — for, flashing through
  Six hundred leagues of water,
Old Mother England's benison
  Salutes her eldest daughter!

O'er all the land the tidings speed,
  And soon, in every nation,
They'll hear about the cable with
  Profoundest admiration!

Now long live James, and long live Vic,
  And long live gallant Cyrus;
And may his courage, faith, and zeal
  With emulation fire us;

And may we honor evermore
  The manly, bold, and stable;
And tell our sons, to make them brave,
  How Cyrus laid the cable!

THE JOLLY MARINER.

A BALLAD.

It was a jolly mariner
  As ever hove a log;
He wore his trousers wide and free,
  And always ate his prog,
And blessed his eyes, in sailor-wise,
  And never shirked his grog.

Up spoke this jolly mariner,
  Whilst walking up and down:—
'The briny sea has pickled me,
  And done me very brown;
But here I goes, in these here clo'es,
  A-cruising in the town!'

The first of all the curious things
  That chanced his eye to meet,
As this undaunted mariner
  Went sailing up the street,
Was, tripping with a little cane,
  A dandy all complete!

He stopped, — that jolly mariner, —
  And eyed the stranger well: —
'What that may be,' he said, says he
  'Is more than I can tell;
But ne'er before, on sea or shore,
  Was such a heavy swell!'

He met a lady in her hoops,
  And thus she heard him hail: —
'Now blow me tight! — but there 's a sight
  To manage in a gale!
I never saw so small a craft
  With such a spread o' sail!

'Observe the craft before and aft, —
  She 'd make a pretty prize!'
And then in that improper way
  He spoke about his eyes,
That mariners are wont to use
  In anger or surprise.

He saw a plumber on a roof,
  Who made a mighty din: —
'Shipmate, ahoy!' the rover cried,
  'It makes a sailor grin
To see you copper-bottoming
  Your upper decks with tin!'

He met a yellow-bearded man,
  And asked about the way;
But not a word could he make out
  Of what the chap would say,

Unless he meant to call him names,
  By screaming, 'Nix furstay!'

Up spoke this jolly mariner,
  And to the man said he,
'I have n't sailed these thirty years
  Upon the stormy sea,
To bear the shame of such a name
  As I have heard from thee!

'So take thou that!' — and laid him flat:
  But soon the man arose,
And beat the jolly mariner
  Across his jolly nose,
Till he was fain, from very pain,
  To yield him to the blows.

'T was then this jolly mariner,
  A wretched jolly tar,
Wished he was in a jolly-boat
  Upon the sea afar,
Or riding fast, before the blast,
  Upon a single spar!

'T was then this jolly mariner
  Returned unto his ship,
And told unto the wondering crew
  The story of his trip,
With many oaths and curses, too,
  Upon his wicked lip! —

As hoping — so this mariner
  In fearful words harangued —
His timbers might be shivered, and
  His le'ward scuppers danged,
(A double curse, and vastly worse
  Than being shot or hanged!)

If ever he — and here again
  A dreadful oath he swore —
If ever he, except at sea,
  Spoke any stranger more,
Or like a son of — something — went
  A-cruising on the shore!

YE TAILYOR-MAN.

A CONTEMPLATIVE BALLAD.

RIGHT jollie is ye tailyor-man,
  As annie man may be;
And all ye daye upon ye benche
  He worketh merrilie.

And oft ye while in pleasante wise
  He coileth up his lymbes,
He singeth songs ye like whereof
  Are not in Watts his hymns.

And yet he toileth all ye while
  His merrie catches rolle;
As true unto ye needle as
  Ye needle to ye pole.

What cares ye valiant tailyor-man
  For all ye cowarde feares?
Against ye scissors of ye Fates
  He pointes his mightie sheares.

He heedeth not ye anciente jests
  That witlesse sinners use;
What feareth ye bolde tailyor-man
  Ye hissinge of a goose?

He pulleth at ye busie threade,
  To feede his lovinge wife
And eke his childe ; for unto them
  It is ye threade of life.

He cutteth well ye riche man's coate,
  And with unseemlie pride
He sees ye little waistcoate in
  Ye cabbage bye his side.

Meanwhile ye tailyor-man his wife,
  To labor nothinge loth,
Sits bye with readie hande to baste
  Ye urchin and ye cloth.

Full happie is ye tailyor-man,
  Yet is he often tried,
Lest he, from fullnesse of ye dimes,
  Wax wanton in his pride.

Full happie is ye tailyor-man,
  And yet he hath a foe,
A cunninge enemie that none
  So well as tailyors knowe.

It is ye slipperie customer
  Who goes his wicked wayes,
And weares ye tailyor-man his coate
  But never, never payes!

TOWN AND COUNTRY.

AN ECLOGUE.

CLOVERTOP.

I 'VE thought, my Cousin, it 's extremely queer
That you, who love to spend your August here,
Don't bring, at once, your wife and children down,
And quit, for good, the noisy, dusty town.

SHILLINGSIDE.

Ah! simple swain, this sort of life may do
For such a verdant Clovertop as you,
Content to vegetate in summer air,
And hibernate in winter — like a bear!

CLOVERTOP.

Here we have butter pure as virgin gold,
And milk from cows that can a tail unfold
With bovine pride; and new-laid eggs, whose praise
Is sung by pullets with their morning lays;
Trout from the brook; good water from the well;
And other blessings more than I can tell!

SHILLINGSIDE.

There, simple rustic, we have nightly plays,
And operatic music, — charming ways
Of spending time and money, — lots of fun;
The Central Park — whene'er they get it done;
Barnum's Museum, full of things erratic,
Terrene, amphibious, airy, and aquatic!

CLOVERTOP.

Here we have rosy, radiant, romping girls,
With lips of rubies, and with teeth of pearls;
I dare not mention half their witching charms;
But, ah! the roundness of their milky arms,
And, oh! what polished shoulders they display,
Bending o'er tubs upon a washing-day!

SHILLINGSIDE.

There we have ladies most superbly made
(By fine *artistes*, who understand their trade),
Who dance the German, flirt a graceful fan,
And speak *such* French as no Parisian can;
Who sing much louder than your country thrushes,
And wear (thank Phalon!) far more brilliant
Blushes!

CLOVERTOP.

Here, boastful Shilling, we have flowery walks,
Where you may stroll, and hold delightful talks,
(No saucy placard frowning as you pass,
'Ten dollars' fine for walking on the grass!')
Dim-lighted groves, where love's delicious words
Are breathed to music of melodious birds.

SHILLINGSIDE.

There, silly Clover, dashing belles we meet,
Sweeping with silken robes the dusty street;
May gaze into their faces as they pass,
Beneath the rays of dimly-burning gas,
Or, standing at a crossing when it rains,
May see some pretty ankles for our pains.

CLOVERTOP.

Here you may angle for the speckled trout,
Play him awhile, with gentle hand, about,
Then, like a sportsman, pull the fellow out!

SHILLINGSIDE.

There, too, is fishing quite as good, I ween,
Where careless, gaping gudgeons oft are seen,
Rich as yon pasture, and almost as green!

CLOVERTOP.

Here you may see the meadow's grassy plain,
Ripe, luscious fruits, and shocks of golden grain;
And view, luxuriant in a hundred fields,
The gorgeous wealth that bounteous Nature yields!

SHILLINGSIDE.

There you may see Trade's wondrous strength and pride,
Where merchant-navies throng on every side,
And view, collected in Columbia's mart,
Alike the wealth of Nature and of Art!

N

CLOVERTOP.

Cease, clamorous cit! I love these quiet nooks,
Where one may sleep, or dawdle over books,
Or, if he wish of gentle love to dream,
May sit and muse by yonder babbling stream—

SHILLINGSIDE.

Dry up your babbling stream! my Clovertop—
You 're getting garrulous; it 's time to stop.
I love the city, and the city's smoke;
The smell of gas; the dust of coal and coke;
The sound of bells; the tramp of hurrying feet;
The sight of pigs and Paphians in the street;
The jostling crowd; the never-ceasing noise
Of rattling coaches, and vociferous boys;
The cry of 'Fire!' and the exciting scene
Of heroes running with their mad 'mersheen;'
Nay, now I think that I could even stand
The direful din of Barnum's brazen band,
So much I long to see the town again!
Good-bye! I 'm going by the evening train!
Don't fail to call whene'er you come to town,
We 'll do the city, boy, and do it brown;
I 've really had a pleasant visit here,
And mean to come again another year.

MY FAMILIAR.

Ecce iterum Crispinus!

I.

Again I hear that creaking step!—
He 's rapping at the door!—
Too well I know the boding sound
That ushers in a bore.
I do not tremble when I meet
The stoutest of my foes,
But Heaven defend me from the friend
Who comes — but never goes!

II.

He drops into my easy-chair,
And asks about the news;
He peers into my manuscript,
And gives his candid views;
He tells me where he likes the line,
And where he 's forced to grieve;
He takes the strangest liberties, —
But never takes his leave!

III.

He reads my daily paper through
  Before I 've seen a word;
He scans the lyric (that I wrote)
  And thinks it quite absurd;
He calmly smokes my last cigar,
  And coolly asks for more;
He opens everything he sees —
  Except the entry door!

IV.

He talks about his fragile health,
  And tells me of the pains
He suffers from a score of ills
  Of which he ne'er complains;
And how he struggled once with death
  To keep the fiend at bay;
On themes like those away he goes —
  But never goes away!

V.

He tells me of the carping words
  Some shallow critic wrote;
And every precious paragraph
  Familiarly can quote;
He thinks the writer did me wrong;
  He 'd like to run him through!
He says a thousand pleasant things —
  But never says 'Adieu!'

VI.

Whene'er he comes — that dreadful man —
  Disguise it as I may,
I know that, like an Autumn rain,
  He 'll last throughout the day.
In vain I speak of urgent tasks;
  In vain I scowl and pout;
A frown is no extinguisher, —
  It does not put him out!

VII.

I mean to take the knocker off,
  Put crape upon the door,
Or hint to John that I am gone
  To stay a month or more.
I do not tremble when I meet
  The stoutest of my foes,
But Heaven defend me from the friend
  Who never, never goes!

HOW THE LAWYERS GOT A PATRON SAINT.

A LEGEND OF BRETAGNE.

A LAWYER of Brittany, once on a time,
  When business was flagging at home,
Was sent as a legate to Italy's clime,
  To confer with the Father at Rome.

And what was the message the minister brought?
  To the Pope he preferred a complaint
That each other profession a Patron had got,
  While the Lawyers had never a Saint!

'Very true," said his Holiness, — smiling to find
  An attorney so civil and pleasant, —
'But my very last Saint is already assigned,
  And I can't make a new one at present.

'To choose from the *Bar* it were fittest, I think;
  Perhaps you've a man in your eye;' —
And his Holiness here gave a mischievous wink
  To a Cardinal sitting near by.

But the lawyer replied, in a lawyer-like way,
  "I know what is modest, I hope;
I did n't come hither, allow me to say,
  To proffer advice to the Pope!"

'Very well,' said his Holiness, 'then we will do
The best that may fairly be done;
It don't seem exactly the thing, it is true,
That the Law should be Saint-less alone.

'To treat your profession as well as I can,
And leave you no cause of complaint,
I propose, as the only quite feasible plan,
To give you a second-hand Saint.

'To the neighboring church you will presently go,
And this is the plan I advise: —
First, say a few *aves* — a hundred or so —
Then, carefully bandage your eyes;

'Then (saying more *aves*) go groping around,
And, touching one object alone,
The Saint you are seeking will quickly be found,
For the first that you touch is your own.'

The lawyer did as his Holiness said,
Without an omission or flaw;
Then, taking the bandages off from his head,
What do you think he saw?

There was St. Michael (figured in paint)
Subduing the Father of Evil;
And the lawyer, exclaiming 'Be *thou* our Saint!'
Was touching the form of the DEVIL!

THE KING AND THE COTTAGER.

A PERSIAN LEGEND.

I.

PRAY list unto a legend
  The ancient poets tell;
'T is of a mighty monarch
  In Persia once did dwell;
A mighty queer old monarch
  Who ruled his kingdom well.

II.

'I must build another palace,'
  Observed this mighty King;
'For this is getting shabby
  Along the southern wing;
And, really, for a monarch,
  It is n't quite the thing.

III.

'So I will have a new one,
  Although I greatly fear,
To build it just to suit me,
  Will cost me rather dear;
And I 'll choose, God wot, another spot,
  Much finer than this here.'

IV.

So he travelled o'er his kingdom
  A proper site to find,
Where he might build a palace
  Exactly to his mind,
All with a pleasant prospect
  Before it, and behind.

V.

Not long with this endeavor
  The King had travelled round,
Ere, to his royal pleasure,
  A charming spot he found;
But an ancient widow's cabin
  Was standing on the ground.

VI.

'Ah, here,' exclaimed the monarch,
  'Is just the proper spot,
If this woman would allow me
  To remove her little cot."
But the beldam answered plainly,
  She had rather he would not!

VII.

'Within this lonely cottage,
  Great Monarch, I was born;
And only from this cottage
  By Death will I be torn:
So spare it, in your justice,
  Or spoil it in your scorn!'

VIII.

Then all the courtiers mocked her,
 With cruel words and jeers: —
' 'T is plain her royal master
 She neither loves nor fears;
We would knock her ugly hovel
 About her ugly ears!

IX.

'When ever was a subject
 Who might the King withstand?
Or deem his spoken pleasure
 As less than his command?
Of course he 'll rout the beldam,
 And confiscate her land!'

X.

But, to their deep amazement,
 His Majesty replied:
'Good woman, never heed them,
 The *King* is on your side:
Your cottage is your castle,
 And here you shall abide.

XI.

'To raze it in a moment,
 The power is mine, I grant;
My absolute dominion
 A hundred poets chant;
For being *Khan* of Persia,
 There 's nothing that I *can't!*

XII.

('T was in this pleasant fashion
The mighty monarch spoke;
For kings have merry fancies
Like other mortal folk:
And none so high and mighty
But loves his little joke.)

XIII.

'But power is scarcely worthy
Of honor or applause,
That in its domination
Contemns the widow's cause,
Or perpetrates injustice
By trampling on the laws.

XIV.

'That I have wronged the meanest
No honest tongue may say:
So bide you in your cottage,
Good woman, while you may;
What 's yours by deed and purchase
No man may take away.

XV.

'And I will build beside it,
For though your cot may be
In such a lordly presence
No fitting thing to see,
If it honor not my castle,
It will surely honor me!

XVI.

'For so my loyal people,
  Who gaze upon the sight,
Shall know that in oppression
  I do not take delight;
Nor hold a king's convenience
  Before a subject's right!"

XVII.

Now from his spoken purpose
  The King departed not;
He built the royal dwelling
  Upon the chosen spot,
And there they stood together,
  The palace and the cot!

XVIII.

Sure such unseemly neighbors
  Were never seen before;
'His Majesty is doting,'
  His silly courtiers swore;
But all true loyal subjects,
  They loved the King the more

XIX.

Long, long he ruled his kingdom
  In honor and renown;
But danger ever threatens
  The head that wears a crown,
And Fortune, tired of smiling,
  For once put on a frown.

XX.

For ever secret Envy
  Attends a high estate;
And ever lurking Malice
  Pursues the good and great;
And ever base Ambition
  Will end in deadly Hate!

XXI.

And so two wicked courtiers,
  Who long had strove in vain,
By craft and evil counsels,
  To mar the monarch's reign,
Contrived a scheme infernal
  Whereby he should be slain!

XXII.

But as all deeds of darkness
  Are wont to leave a clew
Before the glaring sunlight
  To bring the knaves to view,
That sin may be rewarded,
  And Satan get his due, —

XXIII.

To plan their wicked treason,
  They sought a lonely spot
Behind the royal palace,
  Hard by the widow's cot,
Who heard their machinations,
  And straight revealed the plot!

XXIV.

'I see,' — exclaimed the Persian, —
  'The just are wise alone;
Who spares the rights of others
  May chance to guard his own;
The widow's humble cottage
  Has propped a monarch's throne!

LOVE AND LUCRE.

AN ALLEGORY.

LOVE and LUCRE met one day,
In chill November weather,
And so, to while the time away,
They held discourse together.

LOVE at first was rather shy,
As thinking there was danger
In venturing so very nigh
The haughty-looking stranger.

But LUCRE managed to employ
Behavior so potential,
That, in a trice, the bashful boy
Grew bold and confidential.

'I hear,' quoth LUCRE, bowing low,
'With all your hearts and honey,
You sometimes suffer — is it so? —
For lack of mortal money.'

Love owned that he was poor in aught
  Except in golden fancies,
And ne'er as yet had given a thought
  To mending his finances;

'Besides, I 've heard' — so Love went on,
  The other's hint improving —
'That gold, however sought or won,
  Is not a friend to loving.'

'An arrant lie! — as you shall see, —
  Full long ago invented,
By knaves who know not you nor me,
  To tickle the demented.'

And Lucre waved his wand, and lo!
  By magical expansion,
Love saw his little hovel grow
  Into a stately mansion!

And where, before, he used to sup
  Untended in his cottage,
And grumble o'er the earthen cup
  That held his meagre pottage, —

Now, smoking viands crown his board,
  And many a flowing chalice;
His larder was with plenty stored,
  And beauty filled the palace!

And LOVE, though rather lean at first,
  And tinged with melancholy,
On generous wines and puddings nursed,
  Grew very stout and jolly!

Yet, mindful of his early friend,
  He never turns detractor,
But prays that blessings may attend
  His worthy benefactor;

And when his friends are gay above
  Their evening whist or *eucre*,
And drink a brimming health to LOVE,
  He drinks 'success to LUCRE!'

DEATH AND CUPID.

AN ALLEGORY.

AH ! — who but oft hath marvelled why
The gods who rule above
Should e'er permit the young to die,
The old to fall in love !

Ah ! — why should hapless human kind
Be punished out of season ?
Pray listen, and perhaps you 'll find
My rhyme may give the reason.

DEATH, strolling out one Summer's day,
Met CUPID, with his sparrows ;
And, bantering in a merry way,
Proposed a change of arrows !

' Agreed !' — quoth CUPID, — ' I foresee
The queerest game of errors ;
For you the King of Hearts will be !
And I 'll be King of Terrors !'

And so 't was done ; — alas the day
  That multiplied their arts ! —
Each from the other bore away
  A portion of his darts ! —

And that explains the reason why,
  Despite the gods above,
The young are often doomed to die ;
  The old to fall in love !

THE FAMILY MAN.

I ONCE was a jolly young beau,
And knew how to pick up a fan,
But I 've done with all that, you must know,
For now I 'm a family man!

When a partner I ventured to take,
The ladies all favored the plan;
They vowed I was certain to make
'Such an excellent family man!'

If I travel by land or by water,
I have charge of some Susan or Ann;
Mrs. Brown is so sure that her daughter
Is safe with a family man!

The trunks and the bandboxes round 'em
With something like horror I scan,
But though I may mutter, 'Confound 'em!'
I smile — like a family man!

I once was as gay as a templar,
  But levity 's now under ban;
Young people must have an exemplar,
  And I am a family man!

The club-men I meet in the city
  All treat me as well as they can;
And only exclaim, 'What a pity
  Poor Tom is a family man!'

I own I am getting quite pensive;
  Ten children, from David to Dan,
Is a family rather extensive;
  But then — I'm a family man!

NE CREDE COLORI:

OR, TRUST NOT TO APPEARANCES.

THE musty old maxim is wise,
  Although with antiquity hoary;
What an excellent homily lies
  In the motto, '*Ne crede colori!*'

A blustering minion of Mars
  Is vaunting his battles so gory;
You see some equivocal scars,
  And mutter, *Ne crede colori!*

A fellow solicits your tin
  By telling a runaway story;
You look at his ebony skin,
  And think of, *Ne crede colori!*

You gaze upon beauty that vies
  With the rose and the lily in glory,
But certain 'inscrutable dyes'
  Remind you, *Ne crede colori!*

There 's possibly health in the flush
  That rivals the red of Aurora;
But brandy-and-water can blush,
  And whisper, *Ne crede colori!*

My story is presently done,
  Like the ballad of good Mother Morey;
But all imposition to shun,
  Remember, *Ne crede colori!*

CLARA TO CLOE.

AN EPISTLE FROM A CITY LADY TO A COUNTRY COUSIN.

DEAR CLOE: — I 'm deeply your debtor,
  (Though the mail was uncommonly slow,)
For the very agreeable letter
  You wrote me a fortnight ago.
I know you are eagerly waiting
  For all that I promised to write,
But my pen is unequal to stating
  One half that my heart would indite.

The weather is terribly torrid;
  And writing 's a serious task;
The new style of bonnet is horrid;
  And so is the new-fashioned *basque;*
The former — but language would fail
  Were its epithets doubly as strong —
The latter is worn with a tail
  Very ugly and tediously long!

And then as to *crinoline* — Gracious!
  If you only could see Cousin Ruth —
The pictures, for once, are veracious,
  And editors utter the truth!

I know you will think it a pity;
  And every one makes such a sneer of it;
But there is n't a saint in the city
  Whose skirts are entirely clear of it!

And then what a fortune of stuff
  To cover the skeleton over! —
Charles says the idea is enough
  To frighten a sensible lover;
And, pretending that *we* are to blame
  For every financial declension,
Swears husbands must soon do the same,
  If wives have another "extension!"

The town is exceedingly dull,
  And so is the latest new farce;
The parks are uncommonly full,
  But beaux are deplorably scarce;
They 're gone to the 'Springs' and the 'Falls,'
  To exhibit their greyhounds and graces,
And recruit at, — what Frederick calls —
  The Brandy-and-Watering Places!

Since my former epistle, which carried
  The news of that curious plot;
Of Miss S. who ran off — and was married;
  Of Miss B. who ran off — and was not, —
There is n't a whisper of scandal
  To keep gentle ladies in humor,
And Gossip, the pleasant old vandal,
  Is dying for want of a rumor! CLARA.

P. S. — But was n't it funny ? —
  Mrs. Jones, at a party last week,
(The lady so proud of her money,
  Of whom you have oft heard me speak,)
Appeared so delightfully stupid,
  When she spoke, through the squeak of her
      phthisic.
Of the statue of Psyche and Cupid
  As 'the *statute of Cuppid and Physic !*' C.

CLOE TO CLARA.

A SARATOGA LETTER.

DEAR CLARA: — I wish you were here:
  The prettiest spot upon earth!
With everything charming, my dear, —
  Beaux, badinage, music, and mirth!
Such rows of magnificent trees,
  Overhanging such beautiful walks,
Where lovers may stroll, if they please,
  And indulge in the sweetest of talks!

We go every morning, like geese,
  To drink at the favorite Spring;
Six tumblers of water apiece,
  Is simply the regular thing;
For such is its wonderful virtue,
  Though rather unpleasant at first,
No quantity ever can hurt you,
  Unless you should happen to burst!

And then, what a gossiping sight!
  What talk about William and Harry;
How Julia was spending last night;
  And *why* Miss Morton should marry!

Dear Clara, I 've happened to see
 Full many a tea-table slaughter;
But, really, scandal with tea
 Is nothing to scandal with water!

Apropos of the Spring — have you heard
 The quiz of a gentleman here
On a pompous M. C. who averred
 That the *name* was remarkably queer?
'The Spring, — to keep it from failing, —
 With wood is encompassed about,
And derives, from its permanent *railing*,
 The title of "Congress," no doubt!'

'T is pleasant to guess at the reason —
 The genuine motive which brings
Such all-sorts of folks, in the season,
 To stop a few days at the Springs.
Some come to partake of the waters,
 (The sensible, old-fashioned elves,)
Some come to dispose of their daughters,
 And some to dispose of — themselves!

Some come to exhibit their faces
 To new and admiring beholders;
Some come to exhibit their graces,
 And some to exhibit their shoulders;
Some come to make people stare
 At the elegant dresses they 've got;
Some to show what a lady may wear,
 And some — what a lady should not!

Some come to squander their treasure
  And some their funds to improve;
And some for mere love of pleasure,
  And some for the pleasure of love;
And some to escape from the old,
  And some to see what is new;
But most — it is plain to be told —
  Come here — because other folks do!

And that, I suppose, is the reason
  Why *I* am enjoying, to-day,
What's called 'the height — of the season'
  In rather the loftiest way.
Good by — for now I must stop —
  To Charley's command I resign, —
So I'm his for the regular hop,
  But ever most tenderly thine, CLOE.

WISHING.

Of all amusements for the mind,
From logic down to fishing,
There is n't one that you can find
So very cheap as 'wishing.'
A very choice diversion too,
If we but rightly use it,
And not, as we are apt to do,
Pervert it, and abuse it.

I wish — a common wish indeed —
My purse were somewhat fatter,
That I might cheer the child of need,
And not my pride to flatter;
That I might make Oppression reel,
As only gold can make it,
And break the Tyrant's rod of steel,
As only gold can break it.

I wish — that Sympathy and Love,
And every human passion,
That has its origin above,
Would come and keep in fashion;

That Scorn, and Jealousy, and Hate.
  And every base emotion,
Were buried fifty fathom deep
  Beneath the waves of Ocean!

I wish — that friends were always true,
  And motives always pure;
I wish the good were not so few,
  I wish the bad were fewer;
I wish that parsons ne'er forgot
  To heed their pious teaching;
I wish that practising was not
  So different from preaching!

I wish — that modest worth might be
  Appraised with truth and candor;
I wish that innocence were free
  From treachery and slander;
I wish that men their vows would mind;
  That women ne'er were rovers;
I wish that wives were always kind,
  And husbands always lovers!

I wish — in fine — that Joy and Mirth,
  And every good Ideal,
May come erewhile, throughout the earth,
  To be the glorious Real;
Till God shall every creature bless
  With his supremest blessing,
And Hope be lost in Happiness,
  And Wishing in Possessing!

RICHARD OF GLOSTER.

A TRAVESTIE.

PERHAPS, my dear boy, you may never have heard
Of that wicked old monarch, KING RICHARD THE
THIRD, —
Whose actions were often extremely absurd;
And who led such a sad life,
Such a wanton and mad life;
Indeed, I may say, such a wretchedly bad life,
I suppose I am perfectly safe in declaring,
There was ne'er such a monster of infamous daring;
In all sorts of crime he was wholly unsparing;
In pride and ambition was quite beyond bearing;
And had a bad habit of cursing and swearing.

I must own, my dear boy, I have more than suspected
The King's education was rather neglected;
And that at *your* school with any two 'Dicks'
Whom your excellent teacher diurnally pricks
In his neat little tables, in order to fix
Each pupil's progression with numeral nicks,
Master RICHARD Y. GLOSTER would often have heard
His standing recorded as, 'Richard — *the third!*'

But whatever of learning his Majesty had,
'T is clear the King's English was shockingly bad.
At the slightest pretence
Of disloyal offence,
His anger exceeded all reason or sense;
And, having no need to foster or nurse it, he
Would open his wrath, then, as if to disperse it, he
Would scatter his curses like College degrees;
And, quite at his ease,
Conferred his '*d-d*'s.'
As plenty and cheap as a young University!

And yet Richard's tongue was remarkable smooth;
Could utter a lie quite as easy as truth;
(Another bad habit he got in his youth;)
And had, on occasion, a powerful battery
Of plausible phrases and eloquent flattery,
Which gave him, my boy, in that barbarous day,
(Things are different now, I am happy to say,)
Over feminine hearts a most perilous sway.
The women, in spite of an odious hump
Which he wore on his back, all thought him a trump:
And just when he 'd played them the scurviest trick,
They 'd swear in their hearts that this crooked old stick, —
This treacherous, dangerous, dissolute Dick,
For honor and virtue beat Cato all hollow;
And in figure and face was another Apollo!

He murdered their brothers,
And fathers and mothers:

And, worse than all that, he slaughtered by dozens
His own royal uncles and nephews and cousins;
And then, in the cunningest sort of orations,
    In smooth conversations,
    And flattering ovations,
Made love to the principal female relations!
'Twas very improper, my boy, you must know,
For the son of a King to behave himself so;
And you'll scarcely believe what the chronicles show
    Of his wonderful wooings,
    And infamous doings;
But here's an exploit that he certainly *did* do —
    Killed his own cousin NED,
    As he slept in his bed,
And married, next day, the disconsolate widow!

I don't understand how such ogres arise,
But beginning, perhaps, with things little in size,
Such as torturing beetles and bluebottle-flies,
Or scattering snuff in a poodle-dog's eyes, —
King Richard had grown so wantonly cruel,
He minded a murder no more than a duel;
He'd indulge, on the slightest pretence or occasion,
In his favorite amusement of Decapitation,
    Until 'Off with his head!'
    It is credibly said,
From his Majesty's mouth came as easy and pat
As from an old constable, 'Off with his hat!'

    One really shivers,
    And fairly quivers,

To think of the treatment of Grey, and Rivers,
And Hastings, and Vaughn, and other good livers,
All suddenly sent, at the tap of a drum,
From the Kingdom of England to Kingdom-Come!
Of Buckingham doomed to a tragical end
For being the tyrant's particular friend;
Of Clarence who died, it is mournful to think,
Of wine that he was n't permitted to drink!
And the beautiful babies of royal blood,
Two little White Roses both nipt in the bud!
And silly Queen Anne — what sorrow it cost her
(And served her right!) for daring to foster
The impudent suit of this Richard of Gloster;
Who, instead of conferring a royal gratuity,
A dower, or even a decent *Anne*-uity,
Just gave her a portion of — something or other
That made her as quiet as Pharaoh's mother!

Ah, Richard! — you 're going it quite too fast;
Your doom is slow, but it 's coming at last;
Your bloody crown
Will topple down,
And you 'll be done uncommonly brown!
Your foes are thick,
My daring Dick,
And Richmond, a prince and a regular brick,
Is after you now with a very sharp stick!

On Bosworth field the armies to-night
Are pitching their tents in each other's sight;
And to-morrow! — to-morrow! -- they 're going to fight!

And now King Richard has gone to bed;
    But e'en in his sleep
    He cannot keep
The past or the future out of his head.
    In his deep remorse,
    Each mangled corse
Of all he had slain, — or, what was worse,
Their ghosts, — came up in terrible force,
And greeted his ear with unpleasant discourse,
    Until, with a scream,
    He woke from his dream,
And shouted aloud for 'another horse!'

Perhaps you may think, my little dear,
King Richard's request was rather queer;
But I'll presently make it exceedingly clear: —
THE ROYAL SLEEPER WAS OVERFED.
I mean to say that, against his habit,
    He'd eaten Welsh-rabbit
With very bad whisky on going to bed.
I 've had the Night-Mare with horrible force,
And much prefer a different horse!

But see! the murky night is gone!
The Morn is up, and the Fight is on!
The Knights are engaging, the warfare is waging,
On the right — on the left, the battle is raging;
    King Richard is down!
    Will he save his crown?
There's a crack in it now! — he's beginning to
    bleed!
Aha! King Richard has lost his steed!

(At a moment like this 't is a terrible need!)
He shouts aloud with thundering force,
And offers a *very* high price for a horse,
But it's all in vain — the battle is done —
The day is lost! — and the day is won! —
And RICHMOND is King! and RICHARD's a corse!

MORAL.

Remember, my boy, that moral enormities
Are apt to attend corporeal deformities.
Whatever you have, or whatever you lack,
Beware of getting a crook in your back;
And, while you're about it, I'd very much rather
You'd grow tall and superb, i. e. copy your father!

Don't learn to be cruel, pray let me advise,
By torturing beetles and bluebottle-flies,
Or scattering snuff in a poodle-dog's eyes.

If you ever should marry, remember to wed
A handsome, plump, modest, sweet-spoken, well-
bred,
And sensible maiden of twenty — instead
Of a widow whose husband is recently dead!
If you'd shun in your naps those horrible *Incubi*,
Beware what you eat, and be careful what drink
you buy;
Or else you may see, in your sleep's perturbations
Some old and uncommonly ugly relations,
Who'll be very apt to disturb your nutations
By unpleasant allusions, and rude observations!

HO-HO OF THE GOLDEN BELT.

ONE OF THE "NINE STORIES OF CHINA,"

VERSIFIED AND DIVERSIFIED.

A BEAUTIFUL maiden was little MIN-NE,
Eldest daughter of wise WANG-KE;
Her skin had the color of saffron tea,
And her nose was flat as flat could be;
And never were seen such beautiful eyes,
Two almond-kernels in shape and size,
Set in a couple of slanting gashes,
And not in the least disfigured by lashes;
　　And then such feet!
　　You'd scarcely meet
In the longest walk through the grandest street,
　　(And you might go seeking
　　From Nanking to Peeking,)
A pair so remarkably small and neat!
　　Two little stumps,
　　Mere pedal lumps,
That toddle along with the funniest thumps,
In China, you know, are reckoned trumps.

The rank of the owner they instantly show forth,
By the classical rule, '*ex pede*,' and so forth.
It seems a trifle, to make such a boast of it;
    But how they *will* dress it,
    And bandage and press it,
By making the least, to make the most of it!

    As you may suppose,
    She had plenty of beaux
Bowing around her beautiful toes,
Praising her feet, and eyes, and nose,
In rapturous verse and elegant prose!
She had lots of lovers, old and young;
There was lofty LONG, and babbling LUNG,
Opulent TIN, and eloquent TUNG,
Musical SING, and, the rest among,
Great HANG-YU and YU-BE-HUNG.

But though they smiled and smirked and bowed,
None could please her of all the crowd;
LUNG and TUNG she thought too loud;
Opulent TIN was much too proud;
Lofty LONG was quite too tall;
Musical SING sung very small;
And, most remarkable freak of all,
Of great HANG-YU the lady made game,
And YU-BE-HUNG she mocked the same,
By echoing back his ugly name!
But the hardest heart is doomed to melt;
Love is a passion that *will* be felt;

And just when scandal was making free
To hint 'what a pretty old maid she 'd be' —
Little MIN-NE,
(Who but she ?)
Married Ho-Ho of the Golden Belt!
A man, I must own, of bad reputation,
And low in purse, though high in station —
A sort of Imperial poor-relation
Who ranked as the Emperor's second cousin,
Multiplied by a hundred dozen;
And, to mark the love the Emperor felt,
Had a pension clear
Of three pounds a-year,
And the honor of wearing a Golden Belt!
And gallant Ho-Ho
Could really show
A handsome face, as faces go
In the Flowery Land where, you must know,
The finest pinks of beauty grow.
He 'd the very widest kind of jaws,
And his nails were like an eagle's claws,
And — though it may seem a wondrous tail —
(Truth is mighty and will prevail!)
He 'd a *queue* as long as the deepest cause
Under the Emperor's chancery laws!

Yet how he managed to win MIN-NE,
The men declared they could n't see;
But all the ladies, over their tea,
In this one point were known to agree: —
Four gifts were sent to aid his plea:

A smoking-pipe with a golden clog,
A box of tea and a poodle dog,
And a painted heart that was all a-flame,
And bore, in blood, the lover's name.

Ah! how could presents pretty as these
A delicate lady fail to please?
She smoked the pipe with the golden clog,
And drank the tea, and ate the dog,
And kept the heart, — and that 's the way
The match was made, the gossips say.

I can't describe the wedding day,
Which fell in the lovely month of May;
Nor stop to tell of the Honey-Moon,
And how it vanished all too soon;
Alas! that I the truth must speak,
And say, that in the fourteenth week,
Soon as the wedding-guests were gone,
  And their wedding-suits began to doff,
MIN-NE was weeping and 'taking on,'
  For *he* had been trying to 'take her off!'
Six wives before he had sent to Heaven,
And being partial to number 'Seven,'
He wished to add his latest pet,
Just, perhaps, to make up the set.
Mayhap the rascal found a cause
Of discontent in a certain clause
In the Emperor's very liberal laws,
Which gives, when a Golden Belt is wed,
Six hundred pounds to furnish the bed;

And if, in turn, he marry a score,
With every wife six hundred more.

First he tried to murder MIN-NE
With a special cup of poisoned tea;
But the lady, smelling a mortal foe,
Cried 'Ho-Ho! —
I 'm very fond of mild Souchong,
But you — my love — you make it too strong!'

At last Ho-Ho, the treacherous man,
Contrived the most infernal plan
Invented since the world began:
He went and got him a savage dog,
Who 'd eat a woman as soon as a frog,
Kept him a day without any prog,
Then shut him up in an iron bin,
Slipped the bolt, and locked him in;
Then giving the key
To poor MIN-NE,
Said, 'Love, there 's something you *must n't* see
In the chest beneath the orange-tree.'

* * * * *

Poor, mangled MIN-NE! with her latest breath,
She told her father the cause of her death;
And so it reached the Emperor's ear,
And his Highness said, 'It is very clear,
Ho-Ho has committed a murder here!'

And he doomed Ho-Ho to end his life
By the terrible dog that killed his wife;

But in mercy (let his praise be sung!)
His thirteen brothers were merely hung,
And his slaves bambooed, in the mildest way,
For a calendar month, three times a day;
And that's the way that Justice dealt
With wicked Ho-Ho of the Golden Belt!

TOM BROWN'S DAY IN GOTHAM.

Qui mores hominum multorum vidit et URBEM.

I'LL tell you a story of THOMAS BROWN —
I don't mean the poet of Shropshire town;
Nor the Scotch Professor of wide renown;
But 'Honest Tom Brown;' so called, no doubt,
Because with the same
Identical name,
A good many fellows were roving about
Of whom the sheriff might prudently swear
That 'honest' with them, was a *non-est* affair!

Now Tom was a Yankee of wealth and worth,
Who lived and throve by tilling the Earth;
For Tom had wrought
As a farmer ought,
Who, doomed to toil by original sinning,
Began — like Adam — at the beginning.
He ploughed, he harrowed, and he sowed;
He drilled, he planted, and he hoed;
He dug and delved, and reaped and mowed.

(I wish I could — but I can't — tell now
Whether he used a subsoil-plough;
Or whether, in sooth, he had ever seen
A regular reaping and raking machine.)

He took most pains
With the nobler grains
Of higher value, and finer tissues
Which, possibly, one
Inclined to a pun,
Would call — like *Harper* — his '*cereal* issues!'
With wheat his lands were all a-blaze;
'T was amazing to look at his fields of maize;
And there were places
That showed *rye*-faces
As pleasant to see as so many Graces.
And as for Hops,
His annual crops,
(So very extensive that, on my soul,
They fairly reached from pole to pole!)
Would beat the guess of any old fogie,
Or — the longest season at Saratoga!
Whatever seed did most abound,
In the grand result that Autumn found,
It was his plan,
Though a moderate man,
To be early running it into the ground;
That is to say,
In another way: —
Whether the seed was barley or hay,
Large or little, or green or gray, —
Provided only it promised to 'pay,' —

He never chose to labor in vain
By stupidly going against the grain,
But hastened away, without stay or stop,
And carefully put it into his crop.
And he raised tomatoes
And lots of potatoes,
More sorts, in sooth, than I could tell;
Turnips, that always turned up well;
Celery, all that he could sell;
Grapes by the bushel, sour and sweet;
Beets, that certainly could n't be beat;
Cabbage — like some sartorial mound;
Vines, that fairly *cu*-cumbered the ground;
Some pumpkins — more than he could house, and
Ten thousand pears; (that 's twenty thousand!)
Fruit of all kinds and propagations,
Baldwins, Pippins, and Carnations,
And apples of other appellations.
To sum it all up in the briefest space,
As you may suppose, Brown flourished apace,
Just because he proceeded, I venture to say,
In the *nulla-retrorsum-vestigi*-ous way;
That is — if you 're not University-bred —
He took Crocket's advice about going ahead.
At all the State Fairs he held a fair station,
Raised horses and cows and his own reputation;
Made butter and money; took a Justice's niche;
Grew wheat, wool, and hemp; corn, cattle, and — rich!
But who would be always a country-clown?
And so Tom Brown
Sat himself down

And, knitting his brow in a studious frown,
He said, says he : —
It 's plain to see,
And I think Mrs. B. will be apt to agree,
(If she don't, it 's much the same to me,)
That I, TOM BROWN,
Should go to town!
But then, says he, what town shall it be?
Boston-town is consid'rably nearer,
And York is farther, and so will be dearer,
But then, of course, the sights will be queerer;
Besides, I 'm told, you 're surely a lost 'un,
If you once get astray in the streets of Boston.
York is right-angled;
And Boston, right-tangled;
And both, I've no doubt, are uncommon new-fangled.
Ah! — the 'SMITHS,' I remember, belong to York,
('T was ten years ago I sold them my pork,)
Good, honest traders — I'd like to know them —
And so — 't is settled — I 'll go to Gotham!

And so Tom Brown
Sat himself down,
With many a smile and never a frown,
And rode, by rail, to that notable town
Which I really think well worthy of mention
As being America's greatest invention!
Indeed, I 'll be bound that if Nature and Art,
(Though the former, being older, has gotten the start,)

In some new Crystal Palace of suitable size
Should show their *chefs-d'œuvre*, and contend for
    the prize,
The latter would prove, when it came to the scratch,
Whate'er you may think, no contemptible match;
For should old Mrs. Nature endeavor to stagger her
By presenting, at last, her majestic Niagara;
Miss Art would produce an equivalent work
In her great, overwhelming, unfinished NEW YORK!

    And now Mr. Brown
    Was fairly in town,
In that part of the city they used to call 'down,'
Not far from the spot of ancient renown
    As being the scene
    Of the Bowling Green,
A fountain that looked like a huge tureen
Piled up with rocks, and a squirt between;
But the 'Bowling' now has gone where they tally
'The Fall of the Ten,' in a neighboring alley;
And as to the 'Green' — why, that you will find
Whenever you see the 'invisible' kind! —
And he stopped at an Inn that's known very well,
'Delmonico's' once — now 'Stevens-Hotel';
(And, to venture a pun which I think rather witty,
There's no better Inn in this Inn-famous city!)

    And Mr. Brown
    Strolled up town,
And I'm going to write his travels down;
But if you suppose *Tom Brown* will disclose

The usual sins and follies of those
Who leave rural regions to see city-shows —
You could n't well make
A greater mistake;
For Brown was a man of excellent sense;
Could see very well through a hole in a fence,
And was honest and plain, without sham or pretence;
Of sharp, city-learning he could n't have boasted,
But he was n't the chap to be easily roasted.
And here let me say,
In a very dogmatic, oracular way,
(And I'll prove it, before I have done with my lay,)
Not only that honesty 's likely to 'pay,'
But that one must be, as a general rule,
At least half a knave to be wholly a fool!

Of pocketbook-dropping, Tom never had heard,
(Or at least if he had, he 'd forgotten the word,)
And now when, at length, the occasion occurred,
For *that* sort of chaff he was n't the bird.
The gentleman argued with eloquent force,
And begged him to pocket the money, of course;
But Brown, without thinking at all what he said,
Popped out the first thing that entered his head,
(Which chanced to be wondrously fitting and true,)
'No — no — my dear Sir — I'll be *burnt* if I do!'
Two lively young fellows, of elegant mien,
Amused him awhile with a pretty machine —
An ivory ball, which he never had seen.

But though the unsuspecting stranger
In the 'patent safe' saw no patent danger,
He easily dodged the nefarious net,
Because 'he was n't accustomed to bet.'

Ah! — here, I wot,
Is exactly the spot
To make a small fortune as easy as not!
That man with the watch — what lungs he has got!
It's 'Going — the best of that elegant lot —
To close a concern, at a desperate rate, —
The jeweller ruined as certain as fate! —
A capital watch! — you may see by the weight —
Worth one hundred dollars as easy as eight —
Or half of that sum to melt down into plate —
(Brown does n't know 'Peter' from Peter the Great)
But then I can't dwell,
I'm ordered to sell,
And mus'n't stand weeping — just look at the shell —
I warrant the ticker to operate well —
Nine dollars! — it's hard to be selling it under
A couple of fifties — it's cruel, by Thunder!
Ten dollars! — I'm offered — the man who secures
This splended — ten dollars! — say twelve, and it's yours!'
'Don't want it' — quoth Brown — 'I don't wish to buy;
Fifty dollars, I'm sure, one could n't call high —
But to see the man *ruined!* — Dear Sir, I declare —
Between two or three bidders, it does n't seem fair;

To knock it off now were surely a sin;
Just wait, my dear Sir, till the people come in!
Allow me to say, you disgrace your position
As Sheriff — consid'ring the debtor's condition —
To sell *such* a watch without more competition!'
And here Mr. Brown
Gave a very black frown,
Stepped leisurely out, and walked farther up town.
To see him stray along Broadway
In the afternoon of a summer's day,
And note what he chanced to see and say;
And what people he meets
In the narrower streets,
Were a pregnant theme for a longer lay.
How he marvelled at those geological chaps
Who go poking about in crannies and gaps,
Those curious people in tattered breeches,
The rag-wearing, rag-picking sons of — ditches,
Who find in the very nastiest niches
A 'decent living,' and sometimes riches;
How he thought city prices exceedingly queer,
The 'busses too cheap, and the hacks too dear;
How he stuck in the mud, and got lost in the question —
A problem too hard for his mental digestion —
Why — in cleaning the city, the city employs
Such a very small *corps* of such very small boys;
How he judges by dress, and accordingly makes,
By mixing up classes, the drollest mistakes.
How — as if simple vanity ever were vicious,
Or women of merit could be meretricious, —

He imagines the dashing Fifth-Avenue dames
The same as the girls with unspeakable names!
An exceedingly natural blunder in sooth,
But, I 'm happy to say, very far from the truth;
For e'en at the worst, whate'er you suppose,
The one sort of ladies can *choose* their beaux,
While, as to the other — but every one knows
What — if 't were a secret — I would n't disclose.

And Mr. Brown
Returned from town,
With a bran new hat, and a muslin gown,
And he told the tale, when the sun was down,
How he spent his eagles, and saved his crown;
How he showed his pluck by resisting the claim
Of an impudent fellow who asked his name;
But paid — as a gentleman ever is willing —
At the old Park-Gate, the regular shilling!

POST-PRANDIAL VERSES.

RECITED AT THE FESTIVAL OF THE PSI UPSILON FRATERNITY, IN BOSTON, JULY 21, 1853.

DEAR Brothers, who sit at this bountiful board,
With excellent viands so lavishly stored,
That, in newspaper phrase, 't would undoubtedly
groan,
If groaning were but a convival tone,
Which it is n't — and therefore, by sympathy led,
The table, no doubt, is rejoicing instead.
Dear Brothers, I rise, — and it won't be surprising
If you find me, like bread, all the better for
rising, —
I rise to express my exceeding delight
In our cordial reunion this glorious night!

Success to 'PSI UPSILON!' — Beautiful name! —
To the eye and the ear it is pleasant the same;
Many thanks to old Cadmus who made us his
debtors,
By inventing, one day, those capital letters

Which still, from the heart, we shall know how to speak
When we 've fairly forgotten the rest of our Greek!

To be open and honest in all that you do;
To every high trust to be faithful and true;
In aught that concerns morality's scheme,
To be more ambitious *to be* than to *seem;*
To cultivate honor as higher in worth
Than favor of fortune, or genius, or birth;
By every endeavor to render your lives
As spotless and fair as your — possible wives;
To treat with respect all the innocent rules
That keep us at peace with society's fools;
But to face every *canon* that e'er was designed
To batter a town or beleaguer a mind,
Ere you yield to the Moloch that Fashion has reared
One jot of your freedom, or hair of your beard, —
All this, and much more, I might venture to teach,
Had I only a 'call' — and a 'license to preach' —
But since I have not, to my modesty true,
I 'll lay it all by — as a layman should do —
And drop a few lines, tipt with Momus's flies,
To angle for shiners — that lurk in your eyes!

May you ne'er get in love or in debt with a doubt
As to whether or no you will ever get out;
May you ne'er have a mistress who plays the coquette,
Or a neighbor who blows on a cracked clarionet;
May you learn the first use of a lock on your door,
And ne'er, like Adonis, be killed by a bore;

Shun canting and canters with resolute force,
(A 'canter' is shocking, except in a horse;)
At jovial parties mind what you are at,
Beware of your head and take care of your hat,
Lest you find that a favorite son of your mother
Has a brick in the one and an ache in the other;
May you never, I pray, to worry your life,
Have a weak-minded friend, or a strong-minded wife;
A tailor distrustful, or partner suspicious;
A dog that is rabid, or nag that is vicious;
Above all — the chief blessing the gods can impart —
May you keep a clear head and a generous heart;
Remember 't is blessèd to give and forgive;
Live chiefly to love, and love while you live;
And dying, when life's little journey is done,
May your last, fondest sigh, be *Psi* UPSILON!

LINES ON MY THIRTY-NINTH BIRTHDAY.

Ah me! — the moments will not stay!
Another year has rolled away;
And June (the second) scores the line
That tells me I am Thirty-nine!

As thus I haste the mile-stones by,
I mark the numbers with a sigh;
And yet 't is idle to repine
I 've come so soon to Thirty-nine!

O, few that roam this world of ours,
To feel its thorns and pluck its flowers,
Have trod a brighter path than mine
From blithe thirteen to Thirty-nine!

Health, home, and friends, (life's solid part,)
A merry laugh, a fresh, young heart,
Poetic dreams, and love divine —
Have I not *these* at Thirty-nine?

O Time! — forego thy wonted spite,
And lay thy future lashes light,
And, trust me, I will not repine
At twice the count of Thirty-nine!

SONNET TO ——.

THINE is an ever-changing beauty; now
  With that proud look, so lofty yet serene
  In its high majesty, thou seem'st a queen,
With all her diamonds blazing on her brow!
Anon I see, — as gentler thoughts arise
  And mould thy features in their sweet control, —
  The pure, white ray that lights a maiden's soul,
And struggles outward through her drooping eyes;
Anon they flash; and now a golden light
  Bursts o'er thy beauty, like the Orient's glow,
  Bathing thy shoulders' and thy bosom's snow,
And all the woman beams upon my sight!
  I kneel unto the queen, like knight of yore;
  The maid I love; the woman I adore!

THE COCKNEY.

It was in my foreign travel,
  At a famous Flemish inn,
That I met a stoutish person
  With a very ruddy skin;
And his hair was something sandy,
  And was done in knotty curls,
And was parted in the middle,
  In the manner of a girl's.

He was clad in checkered trousers,
  And his coat was of a sort
To suggest a scanty pattern,
  It was bobbed so very short;
And his cap was very little,
  Such as soldiers often use;
And he wore a pair of gaiters,
  And extremely heavy shoes.

I addressed the man in English,
  And he answered in the same,
Though he spoke it in a fashion
  That I thought a little lame;

For the aspirate was missing
  Where the letter should have been,
But where'er it was n't wanted,
  He was sure to put it in!

When I spoke with admiration
  Of St. Peter's mighty dome,
He remarked: ''T is really nothing
  To the sights we 'ave at 'ome!'
And declared upon his honor, —
  Though, of course, 't was very queer. —
That he doubted if the Romans
  'Ad the *h*art of making beer!

When I named the Colosseum,
  He observed, ''T is very fair;
I mean, ye know, it *would* be,
  If they 'd put it in repair;
But what progress or *h*improvement
  Can those curst *H*italians 'ope
While they 're *h*under the dominion
  Of that blasted muff, the Pope?'

Then we talked of other countries,
  And he said that he had heard
That *H*americans spoke *H*inglish,
  But he deemed it quite *h*absurd;
Yet he felt the deepest *h*interest
  In the missionary work,
And would like to know if Georgia
  Was in Boston or New York!

When I left the man-in-gaiters,
  He was grumbling, o'er his gin,
At the charges of the hostess
  Of that famous Flemish inn;
And he looked a very Briton,
  (So, methinks, I see him still)
As he pocketed the candle
  That was mentioned in the bill!

LOVE'S CALENDAR.

TO AN ABSENT WIFE.

O, SINCE 't is decreed by the envious Fates,
  All deaf to the clamoring heart,
That the truest and fondest of conjugal mates
  Shall often be sighing apart;

Since the Days of our absence are many and sad,
  And the Hours of our meeting are few;
Ah! what in a case so exceedingly bad,
  Can the deepest philosophy do?

Pray what can we do — unfortunate elves,
  Unconscious of folly or crime —
But make a new Calendar up for ourselves,
  For the better appraisal of time?

And the *Hours* alone shall the Calendar fill,
  (While *Blanks* show their distance apart,)
Just sufficiently near to keep off the chill
  That else might be freezing the heart;

And each Hour shall be such a glorious hour,
Its moments so precious and dear,
That in breadth, and in depth, and in bliss-giving power,
It may fairly be reckoned a year!

AUGUSTA.

"Incedit regina!"

"HANDSOME and haughty!" — a comment that came
From lips which were never accustomed to malice;
A girl with a presence superb as her name,
And charmingly fitted for love — in a palace!
And oft I have wished (for in musing alone
One's fancy is apt to be very erratic)
That the lady might wear — No! I never will own
A thought so decidedly undemocratic! —
But *if* 't were a *coronet* — this I 'll aver,
No duchess on earth could more gracefully wear it;
And even a democrat — thinking of *her* —
Might surely be pardoned for wishing to share it!

YE PEDAGOGUE:

A BALLAD.

I.

RIGHTE learnéd is ye Pedagogue,
Fulle apt to reade and spelle,
And eke to teache ye parts of speeche,
And strap ye urchins welle.

II.

For as 't is meete to soake ye feete,
Ye ailinge heade to mende,
Ye younker's pate to stimulate,
He beats ye other ende!

III.

Righte lordlie is ye Pedagogue
As any turbaned Turke;
For welle to rule ye District Schoole,
It is no idle worke.

IV.

For oft Rebellion lurketh there
In breaste of secrete foes,
Of malice fulle, in waite to pulle
Ye Pedagogue his nose!

V.

Sometimes he heares with trembling feares,
  Of ye ungodlie rogue
On mischieffe bent, with felle intent
  To licke ye Pedagogue!

VI.

And if ye Pedagogue be smalle,
  When to ye battell led,
In such a plighte, God sende him mighte
  To breake ye rogue his heade!

VII.

Daye after daye, for little paye,
  He teacheth what he can,
And bears ye yoke, to please ye folke,
  And ye Committee-man.

VIII.

Ah! many crosses hath he borne,
  And many trials founde,
Ye while he trudged ye district through,
  And boarded rounde and rounde!

IX.

Ah! many a steake hath he devoured,
  That, by ye taste and sighte,
Was in disdaine, 't was very plaine,
  Of Daye his patent righte!

X.

Fulle solemn is ye Pedagogue,
  Amonge ye noisy churls,
Yet other while he hath a smile
  To give ye handsome girls;

XI.

And one, — ye fayrest mayde of all, —
  To cheere his wayninge life,
Shall be, when Springe ye flowers shall bringe
  Ye Pedagogue his wife!

THE LAWYER'S VALENTINE.

I'M notified, — fair neighbor mine, —
  By one of our profession,
That this — the Term of Valentine —
  Is Cupid's Special Session.

Permit me, therefore, to report
  Myself, on this occasion,
Quite ready to proceed to Court,
  And File my Declaration.

I've an Attachment for you, too;
  A legal and a strong one;
O, yield unto the Process, do;
  Nor let it be a long one!

No scowling bailiff lurks behind;
  He'd be a precious noddy,
Who, failing to Arrest the mind,
  Should go and Take the Body!

For though a form like yours might throw
  A sculptor in distraction;
I could n't serve a Capias — no —
  I'd scorn so base an Action!

O, do not tell me of your youth,
  And turn away demurely;
For though you 're very young, in truth,
  You 're not an Infant surely!

The Case is everything to me;
  My heart is love's own tissue;
Don't plead a Dilatory Plea;
  Let 's have the General Issue!

Or, — since you 've really no Defence,
  Why not, this present Session,
Omitting all absurd pretence,
  Give judgment by Confession?

So shall you be my lawful wife;
  And I — your faithful lover —
Be Tenant of your heart for Life,
  With no Remainder over!

ANACREONTIC.

TO A BEAUTIFUL STRANGER.

A GLANCE, a smile, — I see it yet! —
A moment ere the train was starting;
How strange to tell! — we scarcely met,
And yet I felt a pang at parting!

And you — (alas that all the while
'T is *I* alone who am confessing!)
What thought was lurking in your smile
Is quite beyond my simple guessing.

I only know those beaming rays
Awoke in me a strange emotion,
Which, basking in their warmer blaze,
Perhaps might kindle to devotion.

Ah! many a heart as stanch as this,
By smiling lips allured from Duty,
Has sunk in Passion's dark abyss, —
'Wrecked on the coral reefs of Beauty!'

And so, 't is well the train's swift flight
That bore away my charming stranger,
Took her — God bless her! — out of sight,
And me, as quickly, out of danger!

THE CHOICE OF KING MIDAS.

OR, TOO MUCH OF A GOOD THING.

I.

MIDAS, King of Phrygia, several thousand years ago,
Was a very worthy monarch, as the classic annals show —
You may read 'em at your leisure, when you have a mind to doze,
In the finest Latin verses, or in choice Hellenic prose.

II.

Now this notable old monarch, King of Phrygia, as aforesaid,
(Of whose royal state and character there might be vastly more said,)
Though he occupied a palace, kept a very open door,
And had still a ready welcome for the stranger and the poor.

III.

Now it chanced that old *Silenus*, who, it seems, had
lost his way,
Following *Bacchus* through the forest, in the pleasant month of May,
(Which was n't very singular, for at the present day
The followers of *Bacchus* very often go astray —)

IV.

Came at last to good King MIDAS, who received
him in his court,
Gave him comfortable lodgings, and — to cut the
matter short —
With as much consideration treated weary old
Silenus,
As if the entertainment were for *Mercury* or *Venus*.

V.

Now when *Bacchus* heard the story, he proceeded
to the king,
And says he, 'By old *Silenus* you have done the
handsome thing;
He 's my much respected tutor, who has taught me
how to read,
And I 'm sure your royal kindness should receive
its proper meed;

VI.

So I grant you full permission to select your own
reward:
Choose a gift to suit your fancy, — something worthy
of a lord!'

'*Evœ Bacche!*' cried the monarch, 'If I do not
make too bold,
Let whatever I may handle be transmuted into
gold!'

VII.

Midas, sitting down to dinner, sees the answer to
his wish,
For the turbot on the platter turns into a golden fish!
And the bread between his fingers is no longer
wheaten bread,
But the slice he tries to swallow is a wedge of gold
instead!

VIII.

And the roast he takes for mutton fills his mouth
with golden meat,
Very tempting to the vision, but extremely hard to
eat;
And the liquor in his goblet, very rare, select, and old,
Down the monarch's thirsty throttle runs a stream
of liquid gold!

IX.

Quite disgusted with his dining, he betakes him to
his bed;
But, alas! the golden pillow does n't rest his weary
head;
Nor does all the gold around him soothe the mon-
arch's tender skin;
Golden sheets, to sleepy mortals, might as well be
sheets of tin!

X.

Now poor MIDAS, straight repenting of his rash and foolish choice,
Went to *Bacchus*, and assured him, in a very plaintive voice,
That his golden gift was working in a manner most unpleasant;
And the god, in sheer compassion, took away the fatal present.

MORAL.

By this mythologic story we are very plainly told,
That, though gold may have its uses, there are better things than gold;
That a man may sell his freedom to procure the shining pelf:
And that Avarice, though it prosper, still contrives to cheat itself!

WHERE THERE 'S A WILL THERE 'S A WAY.

Aut viam inveniam, aut faciam.

It was a noble Roman,
  In Rome's imperial day,
Who heard a coward croaker,
  Before the Castle, say:
'They 're safe in such a fortress;
  There is no way to shake it!'
'On — on!' exclaimed the hero,
  '*I 'll find a way, or make it!*'

Is *Fame* your aspiration?
  Her path is steep and high;
In vain he seeks her temple,
  Content to gaze and sigh:
The shining throne is waiting,
  But he alone can take it
Who says, with Roman firmness,
  '*I 'll find a way, or make it!*'

Is *Learning* your ambition?
  There is no royal road;
Alike the peer and peasant
  Must climb to her abode:

Who feels the thirst of knowledge,
  In Helicon may slake it,
If he has still the Roman will
  '*To find a way, or make it!*'

Are *Riches* worth the getting?
  They must be bravely sought;
With wishing and with fretting
  The boon cannot be bought:
To all the prize is open,
  But only he can take it,
Who says, with Roman courage,
  '*I'll find a way, or make it!*'

In *Love's* impassioned warfare
  The tale has ever been,
That victory crowns the valiant, —
  The brave are they who win:
Though strong is Beauty's castle,
  A lover still may take it,
Who says, with Roman daring,
  '*I'll find a way, or make it!*

SAINT JONATHAN.

THERE 's many an excellent Saint, —
St. George, with his dragon and lance;
St. Patrick, so jolly and quaint;
St. Vitus, the saint of the dance;
St. Denis, the saint of the Gaul;
St. Andrew, the saint of the Scot;
But JONATHAN, youngest of all,
Is the mightiest saint of the lot!

He wears a most serious face,
Well worthy a martyr's possessing;
But it is n't all owing to grace,
But partly to thinking and guessing;
In sooth, our American Saint,
Has rather a secular bias,
And I never have heard a complaint
Of his being excessively pious!

He 's fond of financial improvement,
And is always extremely inclined
To be starting some practical movement
For mending the morals and mind.

Do you ask me what wonderful labors
  ST. JONATHAN ever has done
To rank with his Calendar neighbors?
  Just listen, a moment, to one:

One day when a flash in the air
  Split his meeting-house fairly asunder,
Quoth JONATHAN, 'Now — I declare —
  They 're dreadfully careless with thunder!
So he fastened a rod to the steeple;
  And now, when the lightning comes round,
He keeps it from building and people,
  By running it into the ground!

Reflecting, with pleasant emotion,
  On the capital job he had done,
Quoth JONATHAN, 'I have a notion
  Improvements have barely begun;
If nothing 's created in vain, —
  As ministers often inform us, —
The lightning that 's wasted 't is plain,
  Is really something enormous?'

While ciphering over the thing,
  At length he discovered a plan
To catch the Electrical King,
  And make him the servant of man!
And now, in an orderly way,
  He flies on the fleetest of pinions,
And carries the news of the day
  All over his master's dominions!

One morning, while taking a stroll,
He heard a lugubrious cry —
Like the shriek of a suffering soul —
In a Hospital standing near by;
Anon, such a terrible groan
Saluted ST. JONATHAN'S ear,
That his bosom — which was n't of stone —
Was melted with pity to hear.

That night he invented a charm
So potent that folks who employ it,
In losing a leg or an arm,
Don't suffer, but rather enjoy it!
A miracle, you must allow,
As good as the best of his brothers,' —
And blessèd ST. JONATHAN now
Is patron of cripples and mothers!

There 's many an excellent Saint, —
St. George, with his dragon and lance;
St. Patrick, so jolly and quaint;
St. Vitus, the saint of the dance;
St. Denis, the saint of the Gaul;
St. Andrew, the saint of the Scot;
But JONATHAN, youngest of all,
Is the mightiest saint of the lot!

SONG OF SARATOGA.

'Pray, what do they do at the Springs?'
  The question is easy to ask;
But to answer it fully, my dear,
  Were rather a serious task.
And yet, in a bantering way,
  As the magpie or mocking-bird sings,
I'll venture a bit of a song
  To tell what they do at the Springs!

Imprimis, my darling, they drink
  The waters so sparkling and clear;
Though the flavor is none of the best,
  And the odor exceedingly queer;
But the fluid is mingled, you know,
  With wholesome medicinal things,
So they drink, and they drink, and they drink,
  And that's what they do at the Springs!

Then with appetites keen as a knife,
  They hasten to breakfast or dine;
(The latter precisely at three;
  The former from seven till nine.)

Ye gods! what a rustle and rush
  When the eloquent dinner-bell rings!
Then they eat, and they eat, and they eat, —
  And that's what they do at the Springs!

Now they stroll in the beautiful walks,
  Or loll in the shade of the trees;
Where many a whisper is heard
  That never is told by the breeze;
And hands are commingled with hands,
  Regardless of conjugal rings;
And they flirt, and they flirt, and they flirt, —
  And that's what they do at the Springs!

The drawing-rooms now are ablaze,
  And music is shrieking away;
Terpsichore governs the hour,
  And Fashion was never so gay!
An arm round a tapering waist —
  How closely and fondly it clings:
So they waltz, and they waltz, and they waltz, —
  And that's what they do at the Springs!

In short — as it goes in the world —
  They eat, and they drink, and they sleep;
They talk, and they walk, and they woo;
  They sigh, and they laugh, and they weep;
They read, and they ride, and they dance;
  (With other unspeakable things;)
They pray, and they play, and they *pay*, —
  And that's what they do at the Springs!

THE PORTRAIT;

A SONNET.

A PRETTY picture hangs before my view;
The face, 'in little,' of a Southern dame,
To me unknown (though not unknown to fame)
Save by the lines the cunning limner drew.
So grandly Grecian is the lady's head,
I took her for Minerva in disguise;
But when I marked the winning lips and eyes,
I thought of Aphrodite, in her stead;
And then I kissed her calm, unanswering mouth
(The *picture* '*s* mine!) as any lover might,
In the deep fervor of a nuptial night,
And envied him who, in the 'Sunny South,'
Calls *her* his own whose *shadow* can impart
Such very sunshine to a Northern heart!

EPIGRAMS.

ON A FAMOUS WATER-SUIT.

My wonder is really boundless
 That among the queer cases we try,
A land-case should often be groundless,
 And a water-case always be dry!

KISSING CASUISTRY.

When Sarah Jane, the moral Miss,
Declares 't is very wrong to kiss,
 I'll bet a shilling I see through it;
The damsel, fairly understood,
Feels just as any Christian should, —
 She 'd rather *suffer* wrong than *do* it!

THE LOST CHARACTER.

Julia is much concerned, God wot,
For the good name — she has n't got;
So mortgagors are often known
To guard the soil they deem their own;
As if, forsooth, they did n't know
The land was forfeit long ago!

REVERSING THE FIGURES.

Maria, just at twenty, swore
That no man less than six feet four
  Should be her chosen one.
At thirty she is glad to fix
A spouse exactly four feet six,
As better far than none!

TO A POETICAL CORRESPONDENT.

Rose hints she is n't one of those
Who have the gift of writing prose;
But poetry is *une autre chose*,
And quite an easy thing to Rose!
As if an artist should decline,
For lack of skill, to paint a sign,
But, try him in the *landscape* line,
You 'll find his genius quite divine!

A DILEMMA.

'Whenever I marry,' says masculine Ann,
'I must really insist upon wedding a *man!*'
But what if the man (for men are but human)
Would be equally nice about wedding a *woman?*

ON A LONG-WINDED ORATOR.

Three Parts compose a proper speech,
(So wise Quintilian's maxims teach,)
But Loquax never can get through,
In *his* orations, more than two.

He does n't stick at the 'Beginning;'
His 'Middle' comes as sure as sinning;
Indeed, the whole one might commend,
Could he contrive to make an '*End!*'

THE THREE WIVES: A JUBILATION.

My *First* was a lady whose dominant passion
Was thorough devotion to parties and fashion;
My *Second*, regardless of conjugal duty,
Was only the worse for her wonderful beauty;
My *Third* was a vixen in temper and life,
Without one essential to make a good wife.
Jubilate! at last in my freedom I revel,
For I'm clear of the World, and the Flesh, and
the Devil!

THE PRESS.

RECITED BEFORE THE LITERARY SOCIETIES OF BROWN UNIVERSITY, 1855.

A WORTHY parson, once upon a time,
Weary of list'ning to the sober rhyme
That, of a winter's evening, chanced to fall
From a young poet in a lecture hall,
His disappointment openly confessed,
And thus his censure to a friend expressed:—
'The poem, Sir, is well enough no doubt,
But so much preaching one could do without;
A little wit had pleased me more by half;
I did n't come to learn, I came to laugh!'

So goes the world; his very soul to save
They will not let poor Harlequin be grave;
But vote him weaker than a vestry-mouse,
Unless, like Samson, he brings down the house!
Alas! to-day, if such a rule prevail,
My sober muse were surely doomed to fail;
Her subject grave demands a serious song,
And trival treatment were ignobly wrong.

Yet let me hope that e'er my song be done,
When satire comes to punish with a pun,
Some pleasant fancy may your hearts beguile,
And win the favor of an answering smile.

I sing the Press; O sweet Enchantress, bring
Fit inspiration for the theme I sing,
The Art of Arts, whose earliest, freshest fame,
With fierce debate, three rival cities claim;
The glorious art, that, scorning humbler birth,
Came at a bound upon the wondering earth,[13]
Full-armed and strong her instant might to prove,
A new Minerva from the brain of Jove!

I marvel not that rival towns dispute
Where first the goddess set her radiant foot;
That blest Mayence, with honest pride, should boast
The wondrous Bible of her wizard Faust;
That Haarlem, jealous of her proper fame,
Erects a statue to her Coster's name;
While Strasburg's cits contemning all beside,
Vaunt their own hero with an equal pride.

How shall the poet venture to explain
Where plodding History labors still in vain
To solve the mystery — the vexing doubt
That only deepens with the deepening shout
Of angry partisans? The Muse essays
The dangerous task, and thus awards the bays:—
Where counter claims the highest merit hide,
If large the gift, 'tis fairest to divide.

Honor to all who shared a noble part
To find, to cherish, or adorn the art;
Honor to him who, with enraptured eye,
First saw the nymph descending from the sky;
Honor to him, whate'er his name or land,
The first to kneel, and kiss her royal hand;
Thrice honored he who, piercing the disguise
That barred her beauty from obtuser eyes,
First gave her shelter, when the dusky maid
Knocked at his door in homely garb arrayed,
And found at length, beyond his hopes or prayers,
He 'd wooed and won an angel unawares!

I sing the Press; alas, 't were much the same
As though the Muse essayed the trump of fame;
Though something harsh and grating in its tone,
She keeps a mightier trumpet of her own, —
The which, while Freedom's banner is unfurled,
Shall swell her pæans through the wondering world!

Strange is the sound when first the notes begin
Where human voices blend with Vulcan's din;
The click, the clank, the clangor, and the sound
Of rattling rollers in their rapid round;
The whizzing belt, the sharp metallic jar,
Like clashing spears in fierce chivalric war;
The whispering birth of myriad flying leaves,
Gathered, anon, in countless motley sheaves,
Then scattered far, as on the wingéd wind,
The mortal nurture of th' immortal mind!

I'm fond of books; 't is pleasant to behold
In various apparel, new and old,
The quaint array of well-adjusted tomes
That grace the mantels of our rural homes;
The Bible, Bunyan, Baxter, and a score
Of colder lights, from Hume to Hannah More;
Ripe with great thoughts and histories, or full
Of pious homilies, devout and dull.
Nor do I scorn those half-forgotten books
That lie neglected in obscurer nooks
Where poets mould, and critic-spiders spin
Their flimsy lines to mock the lines within!
For here the curious questioner may find
The pregnant hint that in some ampler mind
Grew to a thought, and honors now the page
That beams the brightest on the present age.

I love vast libraries; revere the fame
Of all the Ptolemies; and each other name,
Æmilius, Augustus, Crassus Cæsar, all
The old collectors, whether great or small,
Who helped the cause of learning to advance,—
Trajan and Bodley, Charles the Wise of France,
Kings, nobles, knights, who, anxious of renown
Beyond the fame of garter, spur, or crown,
And wisely provident against decay,
(Since parchment lives while marble melts away,)
Reared to their honor literary domes,
And grew immortal in immortal tomes!

Grand are the pyramids, although the stones
Are but the graves of rotten human bones

That bear, alas! nor name, nor crest, nor date
To show the world their former regal state.
Compared with these, how noble and sublime
The garnered excellence of every clime
Reared in vast Pantheons, and finely wrought,
From sill to cap-stone, of immortal thought!

Here, e'en the sturdy democrat may find,
Nor scorn their rank, the nobles of the mind;
While kings may learn, nor blush at being shown
How Learning's patents abrogate their own.
A goodly company and fair to see;
Royal plebeians; earls of low degree;
Beggars whose wealth enriches every clime;
Princes who scarce can boast a mental dime;
Crowd here together like the quaint array
Of jostling neighbors on a market day.
Homer and Milton — can we call them blind? —
Of godlike sight, the vision of the mind;
Shakespeare, who calmly looked creation through,
'Exhausted worlds, and then imagined new;'
Plato the sage, so thoughtful and serene,
He seems a prophet by his heavenly mien;
Shrewd Socrates, whose philosophic power
Xantippe proved in many a trying hour;
And Aristophanes, whose humor run
In vain endeavor to be-'cloud' the sun; [14]
Majestic Æschylus, whose glowing page
Holds half the grandeur of the Athenian stage;
Pindar, whose odes, replete with heavenly fire,
Proclaim the master of the Grecian lyre;

Anacreon, famed for many a luscious line
Devote to Venus and the god of wine.

I love vast libraries; yet there is a doubt
If one be better with them or without, —
Unless he use them wisely, and, indeed,
Knows the high art of what and how to read.
At Learning's fountain it is sweet to drink,
But 't is a nobler privilege to think;
And oft, from books apart, the thirsting mind
May make the nectar which it cannot find.
'T is well to borrow from the good and great;
'T is wise to learn; 't is godlike to create!

There is a story which my purpose suits;
'T is told by Richter of the author *Wuz* —
A poor lone scholar who, in urgent need
(Or so he thought) of learned books to read,
Wept o'er his poverty, lamenting sore,
(The while a catalogue he pondered o'er,)
Of all the charming works that met his eye,
Not one, alas! his meagre purse could buy.
While musing thus, his racked invention brought
To weeping *Wuz* for once a lucky thought:
'Eureka!' cried the scholar, with a roar, —
As Archimedes shouted once before, —
'I have it! — True, my purse is rather scant,
But then this catalogue shows what I want,
And so who cares for poverty or pelf? —
I'll take my pen and write the books myself!'
Where be our authors now? The noble band

Dwindles apace from off the famished land.
Scarce a round dozen, at the best, remain
Of all who once, among the author-train,
Wrote books like scholars; — nor esteemed it hard,
Genius, like Virtue was its own reward.

O gentle Irving! — thou whom every grace
Of wit and learning gave the highest place
In the proud synod of the old *régime*,
In all thy dreaming, didst thou ever dream
To see thy craft a mere mechanic art,
The servile minion of the bookish mart? —
When authorship should be the merest trade,
And men make books as hats and boots are made?
Didst ever dream to see the wondrous day
When the vexed press should spawn the vast array
Of trashy tomes that on the public burst,
So fast, they print the 'Tenth Edition' first?
Thou hast not read them. God forbid! It racks
One's brains enough to see their brazen backs.
Yet thou wilt smile, I know, when thou art told
That with each book the buyer too is 'sold';
That soon the puffing art shall all be vain,
And sense and reason rule the town again.

Sweet to the traveller is the urchin's chimes,
Proclaiming, ''Ere 's your 'Erald, Tribune, Times!
Those lively records of the passing day,
That catch the echo, ere it dies away,
Of battle, bravery, sudden death, and all
That human minds can startle or appall·

Marriage and murder; things of different name,
Alas! that oft the two should be the same!
Letters describing merry rural scenes;
Ship-news, and, often, news for the marines;
Fortune's bright favors, and Misfortune's shocks;
The fall of Hungary and the fall of stocks;
The important page that tells the thrilling tale
How Empires rise, and 'Red Republics' fail;
How England's lion, loitering in his lair,
Essays in vain to fright the Russian bear;
How France, bemoaning the expensive war,
Would give her 'Louis,' to save her *louis-d'or;*
While the poor Turk, whom hapless luck attends,
Cries, 'Gracious Allah! save me from my friends!'
I have a neighbor, of eccentric views,
Who has a mortal horror of the news;
As lessons are to boys, when long and hard;
Spiders, to ladies; censure, to a bard;
To losers, bets; to holders, railway stock;
Lectures to husbands, after ten o'clock;
Bacon to Hebrews, or to Quakers, war;
Squalls to a sailor, or a bachelor;
To Satan prayer-books, or to Islam, wine,
So are 'the papers' to this friend of mine.
You 've but to ask him, in the common way,
The usual question, and to your dismay,
He 'll pour, remorseless, on your tingling ear,
Such streams of satire as you 'll quake to hear.
'The News? — Thank Heaven! — I 'm not the man to know,
I do not take the papers; you can go,

If you possess the patience and the pelf,
And read the lying journals for yourself;
I hate, despise, detest, abhor them all,
Hebdomadal, diurnal, great, and small.
The *News*, indeed! — pray do you call it news
When shallow noddles publish shallow views?
Pray, is it news that turnips should be bred
As large and hollow as the owner's head?
News, that a clerk should rob his master's hoard,
Whose meagre salary scarcely pays his board?
News, that two knaves, their spurious friendship o'er,
Should tell the truths which they concealed before?
News, that a maniac, weary of his life,
Should end his sorrows with a rope or knife?
News, that a wife should violate the vows
That bind her, loveless, to a tyrant spouse?
News, that a daughter cheats paternal rule,
And weds a scoundrel to escape a fool? —
The news, indeed! — Such matters are as old
As sin and folly, rust and must and mould;
Nor fit to publish even when, in sooth,
By merest chance the papers tell the truth!'

So raves my friend, — a worthy man enough,
But in his utterance rather rude and rough;
Fond of extremes, and so exceeding strong,
E'en in the right he 's often in the wrong.
One of those people whom you may have seen,
(You know them always by their nervous mien,)
Who when they go a-fishing in the well
Where Truth, the angel, is supposed to dwell,

So very roughly knock the nymph about,
She kicks the bucket ere she 's fairly out!—
Yet, if they would, the noble lords of print,
E'en from my friend, might take a wholesome hint.

O for a pen with Hogarth's genius rife
To paint the scenes of Editorial life.
The tale, I know, is rather trite and old,
And yet, perchance, it may be freshly told,
As some plain dish, a simple roast or stew,
Takes a new flavor in a French *ragout.*

SCENE — a third story in a dismal court,
Where weary printers just at eight resort;
A dingy door that with a rattle shuts;
Heaps of 'Exchanges,' much adorned with 'cuts;'
Pens, paste, and paper on the table strewed;
Books, to be read when they have been reviewed;
Pamphlets and tracts so very dull indeed
That only they who wrote them e'er will read;
Nine letters, touching themes of every sort,
And one with money — just a shilling short —
Lie scattered round upon a common level.
PERSONS — the Editor; enter, now, the Devil:—
'Please, Sir, since this 'ere article was wrote,
There 's later news perhaps you 'd like to quote:
'The allies storming with prodigious force,
S'*bas*-to-pol is down!' 'Set it up, of course.'
'And, Sir, that murder 's done — there 's only left
One larceny.' 'Pray don't omit the theft.'

'And, Sir, about the mob — the matter 's fat' —
'The mob? — that 's wrong — pray just distribute
that.'
'And here 's an article has come to hand,
A reg'lar, 'rig'nal package' — 'Let *that* stand!'
Exit the imp of Faust, and enter now
A fierce subscriber with a scowling brow; —
'Sir, curse your paper! — send the thing to' —
Well,
The place he names were impolite to tell;
Enough to know the hero of the Press
Cries, 'Thomas, change the gentleman's address!
We 'll send the paper, if the post will let it,
Where the subscriber will be sure to get it!'

Who would not be an Editor? — To write
The magic 'we' of such enormous might;
To be so great beyond the common span
It takes the plural to express the man;
And yet, alas, it happens oftentimes
A unit serves to number all his dimes!
But don't despise him; there may chance to be
An earthquake lurking in his simple 'we!'
In the close precincts of a dusty room
That owes few losses to the lazy broom,
There sits the man; you do not know his name,
Brown, Jones, or Johnson — it is all the same —
Scribbling away at what perchance may seem
An idler's musing, or a dreamer's dream;
His pen runs rambling, like a straying steed;
The 'we' he writes seems very 'wee' indeed;

But mark the change; behold the wondrous power
Wrought by the Press in one eventful hour;
To-night, 't is harmless as a maiden's rhymes;
To-morrow, thunder in the *London Times!*
The ministry dissolves that held for years;
Her Grace, the Duchess, is dissolved in tears;
The Rothschilds quail; the church, the army, quakes;
The very kingdom to its centre shakes;
The Corn Laws fall; the price of bread comes down —
Thanks to the 'we' of Johnson, Jones, or Brown!

Firm in the right, the daily Press should be
The tyrant's foe, the champion of the free;
Faithful and constant to its sacred trust;
Calm in its utterance; in its judgments, just;
Wise in its teaching; uncorrupt, and strong
To speed the right, and to denounce the wrong.
Long may it be ere candor must confess
On Freedom's shores a weak and venal Press.

NOTES.

NOTE 1. Page 7.

'To show, for once, that Dutchmen are not dull.'

Pere Bouhours seriously asked 'if a German could be a "*bel esprit.*" This concise question was answered by Kramer, in a ponderous work entitled '*Vindiciæ nominis Germanicæ.*'

NOTE 2. Page 13.

'In closest girdle, O reluctant Muse,
In scantiest skirts, and lightest stepping-shoes.'

Imitated from the opening couplet of Holmes's 'Terpsichore,'—

'In narrowest girdle, O reluctant Muse,
In closest frock, and Cinderella shoes.'

NOTE 3. Page 13.

'She stoops to conquer in a Grecian curve.'

Terence, who wrote comedies a little more than two thousand years ago, thus alludes to this and a kindred custom *then* prevalent among the Roman girls:—

'Virgines, quas matres student
Demissis humeris esse, vincto corpore, ut graciles fiant.'

T

The sense of the passage may be given in English, with sufficient accuracy, thus:—

Maidens, whom fond, maternal care has graced
With stooping shoulders, and a cinctured waist.

NOTE 4. Page 17.

'Their tumid tropes for simple Buncombe made.'

Many readers, who have heard about 'making speeches for Buncombe,' may not be aware that the phrase originated as follows:—A member of Congress from the county of Buncombe, North Carolina, while pronouncing a magniloquent set-speech, was interrupted by a remark from the chair, that 'the seats were quite vacant.' 'Never mind, never mind,' replied the orator, 'I'm talking for Buncombe!'

NOTE 5. Page 17.

'Till rising high in rancorous debate,
And higher still in fierce, envenomed hate,'
Etc.

'Sed jurgia prima sonare
Incipiunt animis ardentibus; hæc tuba rixæ;
Dein clamore pari concurritur, et vice teli
Sævit nuda manus." — JUV. Sat. xv.

NOTE 6. Page 21.

'Not uninvited to her task she came.'

This Poem was written at the instance of the Associated Alumni of Middlebury College, and spoken before that Society, July 22, 1846.

NOTE 7. Page 21.

'No singer's trick, — conveniently to bring
A sudden cough when importuned to sing.'

The capriciousness of musical folk, here alluded to, is by no means peculiar to our times. A little before the Christian era, Horace had occasion to scold the Roman singers for the same fault: —

'*Omnibus hoc vitium est cantoribus, inter amicos,*
Ut nunquam inducant animum cantare rogati;
Injussi nunquam desistant.' — SAT. III.

NOTE 8. Page 111.

'*While the dear country, as the reader learns,*
Is saved or ruined in quadrennial turns.'

It is certainly very notable that the difference between the country's 'ruin' and 'salvation,' by the vicissitudes of politics, is so little obvious to the mere observer of national affairs, that he would scarcely know when to weep or rejoice, but for the timely information afforded by his party newspaper!

NOTE 9. Page 111.

'*While their own thoughts the wretches fear to speak,*
Not Sundays only, but throughout the week.'

An allusion to the Scriptural injunction, 'not to speak one's own words' on the Sabbath day.

NOTE 10. Page 116.

'*And hush the wail of Peter Plymley's ghost.*'

Rev. Sydney Smith, the English author and wit, lately deceased, who, having speculated in Pennsylvania Bonds to the damage of his estate, berated 'the rascally repudiators' with much spirit, and lamented his losses in many excellent jests.

NOTE 11. Page 116.

'*Unfriendly hills no longer interpose*
As stubborn walls to geographic foes,
Nor envious streams run only to divide
The hearts of brethren ranged on either side.'

'Lands intersected by a narrow frith
Abhor each other. Mountains interposed
Make enemies of nations, who had else
Like kindred drops been mingled into one'

Note 12. Page 118.

'*No pitying nymphs had gathered round to weep.*'

It is a part of the fable of Phaethon, the son of Helios, of whom mention is made a few lines above, that, when he had fallen from the sky and was drowned in the river Eridanus, his sisters, the Heliades, assembling on the shore, lamented his fate in tears, which were changed to amber as they fell.

Note 13. Page 293.

'*Came at a bound upon the wondering earth.*'

It is a notable fact, — as one may see by a glance at the early specimens of printing, — that *typography* was at the very first so excellent as to leave little room for improvement. With equal truth and felicity it has been called, *Ars simul inventa atque perfecta.*'

Note 14. Page 296.

'*Aristophanes, whose humor run*
In vain endeavor to be-"cloud" the sun.'

An allusion to the comedy of "The Clouds," written in ridicule of Socrates.

THE END.

www.ingramcontent.com/pod-product-compliance
Lightning Source LLC
LaVergne TN
LVHW020229110826
845151LV00003B/870

* 9 7 8 1 4 2 5 5 3 1 3 7 9 *